GriefKeeping

By the Author

Grievers Ask (Augsburg)

A Child-Sized Grief (Beacon Hill Press)

Grieving the Death of a Mother (Augsburg)

The Grief Caring Church (Beacon Hill Press)

When Your Friend Dies (Augsburg)

When You Don't Know What to Say: How to Help Your Grieving Friends (Beacon Hill Press)

Finding Your Way to Say Goodbye: Comforting the Dying (Ave Maria Press)

Finding Your Way to Say Goodbye: Comfort for the Dying and Those Who Care for Them (Ave Maria Press)

When Your People Are Grieving: Leading in Times of Loss (Beacon Hill Press)

Friendgrief: An Absence Called Presence (Baywood)

Journaling Your Decembered Grief: To Help You Through Your Loss (Beacon Hill Press)

ABCs of Healthy Grief: Light for a Dark Journey (Shawnee Mission Medical Center)

A Decembered Grief (Beacon Hill Press)

Grieving the Death of a Friend (Augsburg)

Death and Grief: Healing Through the Small Group (Augsburg)

On Grieving the Death of a Father (Augsburg)

A Time for Healing: Coming to Terms with Your Divorce (Lifeway)

Once in a Lifetime (Thomas Nelson)

Singles in the Workplace: Myths and Advantages in Work and Family Issues (American Society of Personnel Administrators)

Tear-Catching: Developing Your Gift of Compassion (Abingdon)

GriefKeeping

Learning How Long Grief Lasts

Harold Ivan Smith

A Crossroad Book
The Crossroad Publishing Company
New York

The Crossroad Publishing Company
16 Penn Plaza, 481 Eighth Avenue
New York, NY 10001

The text is set in 11.5/15 Korinna.
The display font is Calligraphic 421.

Printed in the United States of America

Cataloging-in-Publication Data is available from
the Library of Congress
ISBN 0-8245-2258-3

1   2   3   4   5   6   7   8   9   10   10   09   08   07   06   05   04

GriefKeeping is dedicated to five scholars who have stretched my understanding of grief. They have dared to think beyond the convenience of "stages" and opened the path for me to comprehend the potential of grief keeping. They are encouragers who make time in busy schedules to notice the work of writers like me.

J. William Worden, Ph.D.
Robert Neimeyer, Ph.D.
Phyllis Silverman, Ph.D.
Kenneth Doka, Ph.D.
Charles Corr, Ph.D.

To the grievers who read *GriefKeeping*
Vahayi bruchan ba 'asher tihyi

"And may you be blessed in all that you are."

For everything there is a season,
and a time for every matter under heaven:
a time to be born, and a time to die;
a time to plant, and a time to pluck up what is planted;
a time to kill, and a time to heal;
a time to break down, and a time to build up;
a time to weep, and a time to laugh;
a time to mourn, and a time to dance;
a time to throw away stones,
    and a time to gather stones together;
a time to embrace, and a time to refrain from embracing;
a time to seek, and a time to lose;
a time to keep, and a time to throw away;
a time to tear, and a time to sew;
a time to keep silence, and a time to speak;
a time to love, and a time to hate;
a time for war, and a time for peace.
                    (Ecclesiastes 3:1–8, NRSV)

Contents

The Right to Keep Your Grief

> We must no longer be afraid to challenge a culture
> that expects silence on the subject of death, a cul-
> ture that closets the process and then once death
> happens, asks us to grieve privately and quickly.
> —Barbara K. Roberts, *Death without Denial*[1]

You know that scene in movies when a police detective says, "Read him his rights"? In grief, there is one right that never gets read. You, as a griever, have a right, whatever the loss, not only to grieve your loss, but to keep your grief.

You do not "get over" grief. Anyone who says that you can, or tells you how they did, is not to be believed. Grief keepers accept their grief and weave it into the fabric of their lives.

Some grievers take their cues from mourners in the public eye and seemingly delay, postpone, or mothball their grief. They take to heart admonitions whispered in a funeral home tone to "Be strong," which the heart hears as "Buck-up-and-suck-it-up!" You can almost see some individuals consulting their Day-Timers or Palm Pilots, "Let's see, I can work grief in on the 14th of July, late afternoon."

Grief will not cooperate with any time limit. Grief makes a shambles of priorities, commitments, and responsibilities. Grief is an unruly houseguest that re-arranges the most highly scheduled and disciplined lives. Individuals who try to manage their grief, in a culture that manages anger, weight, and bottom lines, learn that grief is unmanageable. One postpones grief at one's own emotional, physical, and spiritual risk.

~ *Still grieving.* How long will grieving take? As long as it needs to. Try to rush it and see what happens. Admittedly, that is not an acceptable answer in a frantic time-oriented culture that expects a griever to bounce back after even a tragic death. A culture that wants to hear, "Doing fine. It was tough for a while, but we're doing fine."

As I closed the first session of a Grief Gathering at St. Luke's Hospital, I asked if anyone had questions, meaning about how my six-week program worked.

"Yes," a new widow spoke up. "How long before I get over it? Everyone is telling me that I should be over it by now." (Her husband had been dead sixty days.) Nine pairs of eyes turned to me. I felt like the guy on an E. F. Hutton commercial.

"I do not think healthy people 'get over' it. You integrate significant loss into your life. You do not 'get over' it. Look at the inside of your right thumb." They complied. "Notice the lines and ridges. There are 6.2 billion people on planet Earth, and not another one of them — not one! — has a thumbprint like yours. So if the Creator went to that much trouble to make your thumbprint unique, your grief print will be unique, too."

"Thank you for that candid answer," the widow responded.

The next week when the group met and I asked participants why they returned, this widow spoke up: "Because you are the first person to tell me the truth. I wanted to see what else you might have to say."

Making room for grief. "Get over it" is one of the most abrasive phrases in the English language, a phrase that can lash grievers like a cat-of-nine-tails. God help you if the grief patrol concludes that you are not getting over your loss fast enough. I wish someone would create a bumper sticker: "I'm grieving as fast as I can."

Elizabeth Hutchinson Jackson's death of typhus in 1781 left her thirteen-year-old son, Andrew, to fend for himself. His father had died before Andrew was born. Would anyone standing at that grave have predicted future greatness for this bereft boy? One Jackson biographer concluded: "Betty had been the most important person in her son's life — the person who had advised him, admired him, believed in him, encouraged him, protected him against enemies. No one else... could fill those roles. He would revere her memory and cite her as an authority as long as he lived. Certain consequences of her death radiated through the rest of [Andrew] Jackson's life."[2]

The death of his wife, Rachel, weeks after his election in 1828, must have resurrected memories of his grief following his mother's death. President-elect Andrew Jackson stood at his wife's grave a week before Christmas 1828 on the Hermitage plantation near Nashville. When a weeping black slave tried to jump into the grave, she was restrained and admonished. Jackson, surprisingly, challenged those who wanted to squelch her. He allowed the elderly slave "a final moment beside her mistress."[3]

Only sheer emotional discipline kept him from jumping in the grave, too. Six years later, when he was expected to be over it, Peggy Eaton, wife of the secretary of the treasury, found him sprawled on his wife's grave. She did not interrupt his expression of grief.[4]

These days, if a griever is stretched out on a loved one's grave, someone would shout, "Prozac!"

~ *Grieving in your own time.* Barbara Roberts's father, her most loyal supporter, died three weeks before she was elected Oregon's first woman governor in 1990. Grief revisited her two years into her term, when her husband, Frank, died after battling cancer. As governor, in full view of the public, Roberts kept her griefs.

Grief will not be long denied its due. The only question is: Do you choose thorough or lite grief? Too many people resist, protesting, "I don't know how to grieve." Grief demands, not invites, "Grieve!"

I have long appreciated Barbara Lazear Ascher's words, composed after her brother's death, "I have been trying to make the most of grief. Now, I am letting grief make the most of me."[5]

In a disposable society, we discard grief as expediently as possible, but incredible things happen when we keep a grief long enough for it to make us wiser.

~ *Lamenting.* I listened in a Kansas cemetery as a father moaned, "I was supposed to be skiing with my son today. Thursday, I was supposed to have bought him a ski ticket; instead I bought him a casket." Laments are public opportunities to express our feelings about our loved one, honoring their memory and telling others what they contributed to our lives.

In our families, neighborhoods, communities of faith, and workspaces, individuals are anxious to nip public grief in the bud. With all the grace of a Marine drill sergeant, the grief patrols tell us to "Move it, mister."

Full-bloomed grief is a raw reality few want to witness, let alone experience.

In a move-on culture, we have forgotten the old grief ways. Imagine a woman wearing black for a year! Imagine a man wearing a black armband for a year!

~ *Asking God "Why?"* Many grievers are showered with clichés: "He's in a better place," "God never puts more on us than we can handle," "It's not for us to ask, 'Why?'" I continue to be amazed that more individuals are not whacked severely about the head and shoulders after lobbing a cliché at a griever.

Victoria Alexander, following her father's suicide, gave herself permission to grieve. The young woman looked for sources of comfort as well as safe places to engage her grief. Because her father, a Roman Catholic, had committed suicide, he was denied a funeral mass and could not be buried in consecrated soil. Alexander found few safe places to express her sadness and frustration. She insisted that all grievers, regardless of the circumstances or details of their loved one's death, have three rights:

- To find words to wrap around their grief
- To say the words aloud
- To know that their words have been heard[6]

~ *Hoping.* George H. W. Bush's mother, Dorothy Walker Bush, died two weeks after Bill Clinton defeated him. Days after the funeral, relaxing at Kennebunkport for Thanksgiving, out of sight of the media (but not out of sight of the Secret Service), Bush struggled for composure while grieving. Imagine the world's most powerful leader reduced to alternating tears and laughter, so

13

much so that George Bush wondered about the reaction of his Secret Service detail. He wrote in his diary: "Mum left us. It's kind of like our compass is spinning a little. Even when she was tired and failing she was our guide. I walked up by the Bungalow a lot this long Thanksgiving weekend. I found myself choking up. Then I found myself smiling. The agents probably said to each other, 'The old guy's finally lost it.' "[7]

The critical issue is not what you will do *about* your grief. Rather, it is what you will do *with* your grief. Too many people, whatever the loss, try to get over it, to get beyond their grief. Antidepressants, work, alcohol, sex, shopping, travel — all offer reprieves until grief announces: "I'm back!" Give your grief time.

~ *Naming your grief.* Too often, far too often, grievers are interrupted, "Oh, I know what you mean. When my mother (or father or sister or brother or grandmother or whatever) died, I..." How can someone else be sure that they know what you mean if they don't listen to what you have to say? You may not even be sure what you mean yet, and talking about your grief, naming it, can help.

Blessed are you if you have friends who will listen to you as you tell the stories of your loss. Friends who resist the urge to jump in and say something, who offer an alternative to the "get on with it" cultural norm.

~ *Reinventing yourself.* The nation watched an unfolding political drama in Missouri in late October 2000. Party leaders, media pundits, and political commentators speculated on who would take Mel Carnahan's seat in the Senate — should he be elected — after he, his son Randy, and Chris Stafford, a close friend and political aide, were killed in a plane clash. At the time of his death, Governor Carnahan was in a tight race with the incumbent, John Ashcroft.

Jean Carnahan, a seasoned political wife, agreed to accept the appointment should her late husband be elected, and the media was fascinated by the prospects of a dead man being elected to the Senate. When pundits dismissed the effort as a sympathy vote, bumper stickers and campaign buttons appeared reading "I'm still with Mel." And Carnahan won.

Immediately a grieving widow, mother, and grandmother was thrown into a whirlwind of moving to Washington, hiring a staff, selecting housing, and launching a reelection campaign since she could only serve for two years without running for the seat.

Mrs. Carnahan, a senator's wife who reinvented herself as a senator, captured the upheaval in her life succinctly: "Life has not turned out the way it was supposed to."[8]

~ *Grieving family style.* Mark Pinkard died three days after graduating from high school. That jubilant spring night in El Dorado, Arkansas, as he posed in cap and gown for pictures and opened cards and presents, there was no indication that the party would soon be over. He and his well-wishers were looking down the road to future graduations and predicting great things for Mark. Seventy-two hours later, Mark died in a collision with a log truck on a winding road. Parents, sister, grandparents, friends, and classmates were stunned by the young man's death.

Not all family members grieve alike. Keeping a grief can be particularly challenging for a husband and wife grieving the death of a child if they were taught to grieve differently. Even as you read this, in bedrooms across

15

the country grievers lie in darkness examining their grief alone, not sharing it with the person next to them or with another family member.

~ **Remembering.** Kenro Shimamoto kept his grief. In 1971, a helicopter was shot down in Laos, and four photographers covering the Vietnam War died; one of them was Kenro's brother, Keisaburo, a freelancer for *Newsweek.* Years passed. Then in 1998, a United States MIA search team excavated the site.

A newspaper story about the search caught Kenro's attention. In cooperation with the Japanese embassy and the *Yomiuri Shimbun,* a Tokyo newspaper, Kenro traveled to the search site. On that Laotian hillside he conducted a private Buddhist ceremony, pouring sake onto the ground and collecting a handful of soil — symbolic of his brother's remains — and placing it in an urn to be buried in Japan.[9]

On April 17, 1998, on a small island in Western Japan, Kenro, his aged mother, and other family members held a service for Keisaburo and interred the urn containing the symbolic remains. Twenty-seven years is not too long to keep a grief.

~ **Modeling pride in grief keeping.** Blessed are those who find permission to keep their grief. Especially those who are able to grieve in their own time. Two thousand years ago, Jesus said, "Blessed are those who mourn, for they shall be comforted."[10] Few verses of sacred text sound so outrageous in our society. Those who grieve in contemporary American culture often find themselves alienated and critiqued rather than comforted.

Jesus did not link the promised comfort with a time frame. Most grievers want a "now" clause, like a sixty-day money-back guarantee: "Blessed are those who grieve for they shall be comforted within sixty days." Jesus promised only that comfort will come.

We do not "get over" grief simply to be done with it. Rather, we grow through grief as apprentices, gathering wisdom and skills that can only be learned by taking our time and keeping our grief.

On the long journey to a far place, give yourself permission to keep your grief.

You Have Permission to Grieve
as Long as You Need

Life is too precious and grieving is too important to permit the delegation of dying and mourning to a closeted experience.

—Barbara Roberts, *Death without Denial*[1]

Since boyhood, brothers Fred, Bob, and Paul Westerlund wondered what had happened to their father, a crew member of the USS *Eagle,* a submarine chaser that exploded and broke apart south of Portland, Maine, in May 1945. Forty-nine sailors died that night. Although the U.S. Navy identified a boiler explosion as the cause, rumors persisted about a German U-boat attack.

The truth might never have been known had two of the brothers not told the story about their father's death in a bar one night. The story intrigued Paul Lawton, a lawyer, military historian, and submarine enthusiast. Their mother, who had never believed the Navy report, told them that survivors had glimpsed a submarine conning tower marked with a red horse trotting on a yellow shield. That detail intrigued the naval historian. If the USS *Eagle* had been torpedoed by a German sub, Westerlund and the other men on board would have been entitled to military honors. Instead, the sailors of the *Eagle* had been written off as victims of an unfortunate accident.

Consulting a definitive text on U-boats by Jürgen Rohwer, a German naval historian, Lawton made a startling discovery: Rohwer thought that a German U-353 had sunk the USS *Eagle*. If so, why would the government contend a boiler had exploded? Pursuing key documents, Lawton discovered that the files on the incident were missing.

After the Westerlund brothers ran an ad in the *Boston Globe* asking survivors to contact them, John Breeze called and confirmed that he had seen the dark silhouette of a submarine in the water that night. A second caller, Alice Hultgren, who had taken notes at a hastily convened naval court of inquiry, remembered, "The fellows all said there had been a sub."

Everywhere Paul Lawton searched, he was stonewalled until the seventy-six-page Court of Inquiry Report mysteriously arrived in his mail in October 1999. After reading it, Lawton concluded that naval officers had dismissed the testimony of the survivors to hide a security breach: a German submarine had penetrated American waters in wartime. Lawton's interest attracted the support of Bernard Cavalcante, a naval archivist who had worked with Rohwer. Cavalcante decided it was past time for the official truth to give the men of the USS *Eagle* the respect, admittedly delayed, of a grateful nation.

On June 2, 2002, forty-seven years after the USS *Eagle* sunk, aboard the USS *Salem* — a naval museum ship docked in Quincy, Massachusetts — the families gathered for the awarding of Purple Hearts to crew members. Paul, Bob, and Fred and their mother, Phyllis, received their father's Purple Heart. More significantly, the brothers met three survivors who had been the last to see their father alive.[2]

Since that horrible night in 1945, Harold Petersen, seventy-nine, had carried a burden. Petersen told a reporter for the *Boston Herald,* "You carry that on your shoulder for years. Did I do something? Were we negligent? Did we kill all those men?" Petersen knew that before leaving the engine room that night, he had checked all the critical gauges.[3] Jack Scagneli said, "It weighed on me. I'm extremely happy that it was not a mechanical failure. I feel sad for the families that lost sons. I hope it gives them some comfort that it was enemy action and not somebody's fault."[4] Unfortunately, hundreds of parents and family members died before the Navy admitted the cover-up.

The writer of Ecclesiasticus advised, "Let grief end with the funeral; a life of grief oppresses the mind. Do not abandon your heart to grief."[5] The Westerlunds, however, challenged the mandate to "get over it" and waited for the truth.

Ministers and mourning. As a result of the widespread dissemination of Elisabeth Kübler-Ross's work on death and dying, we have an easily explainable five-stage template for grief: denial, anger, bargaining, depression, and acceptance (or some variation thereof). There are many who declare that if you do the stages "correctly," you will get over your grief with minimal inconvenience.

Some ministers adapted such thinking to any loss; one theory fits all! In an article entitled, "The Mourning After: 10 Steps to Be Healed from the Wound of Grief," the author outlined a string of survivor's attitudes:

- I will vividly examine the future.

- I will not be defeated.

- I will take advantage of available opportunities.

- I will not assume the victim posture.

The author gushed: "By taking these steps, you ensure that you will have a healthy bereavement and that you will complete the grief process. Like others before you, you will make the transition from anxiety to acceptance and from pain to peace. You will, in fact, heal from the deep wound of grief."[6] Work the affirmations and you, too, can live happily ever after. All that was missing in the article was the money-back guarantee.

Some ministers, frustrated with a still-grieving congregant, will unleash the article's concepts upon that griever under the guise of pastoral care. Hope Edelman rejected such pragmatic thinking in our fix-it society: "Here's what I've learned about grief: It's not linear. It's not predictable. It's anything but smooth and self-controlled. Someone did us all a grave injustice by implying that mourning has a distinct beginning, middle, and end. That's the stuff of short fiction. It's not life."[7]

I want to carve Edelman's words on a large monument at the entrance to every cemetery in this country. I doubt that Phyllis Westerlund, holding her husband's Purple Heart, mumbled, "Finally, all done." By keeping their grief, the Westerlunds helped others unlock the mystery of the sinking of the USS *Eagle.*

~ *Using music to grieve.* Historically, grief was kept through singing. My maternal grandfather had a reputation as a funeral singer in his Indiana farm community. He and some friends often left their fields to go sing

21

"a good song" about reunion with family and friends in heaven.

A good mournful funeral song makes you feel sad and good at the same time.

Shifting services from communities of worship to funeral home chapels has turned attendees into passive spectators. Rarely do services in funeral homes include congregational singing. These days, some "memorable experience arrangers" urge grievers not to select favorite music because "you'll be sad every time you hear it."

Anthems remind some grievers of previous grief rituals. In my parish, the choirmaster places notes on the hymns in the worship folder. One Sunday we sang a hymn I had never heard before, "Lord, Whose Love through Humble Service." With grief that was raw after my mother's death, I was ambushed by the hymn text:

> Still your children wander homeless;
> Still the hungry cry for bread;
> Still the captives long for freedom;
> Still in grief we mourn our dead.[8]

I stopped singing. I could not see the hymnal for my tears. The hymn was describing me! "Still in grief we mourn our dead" reverberated along the corridors of my heart long after the service ended. Through a hymn, I was given permission to still grieve.

Hymnologist Brian Wren contends that early Christians, aglow with Easter and the anticipation of personal resurrection, slowly abandoned the long Jewish heritage of lament found in the psalms. Any remnant of lament was lost at the Reformers' insistence on the absolute sovereignty of God: "You got a problem with grief, buddy, you got a problem with God!" According to Wren, "In popular theology, the argument is a slam dunk: since God's sovereignty is absolute, suffering cannot be questioned. It must be God's will. Thus, when evil and suffering overwhelm us, the last thing we permit ourselves to do is complain, still less rage against God. Instead, we 'trust and obey, for there's no other way, to be happy in Jesus.' "[9]

Besides, some demand, why are you singing sad songs and keeping grief when your loved one is singing with the angels? I was stunned when Dr. Phil told a "still grieving father" that his tears were putting out his white-robed son's candle in heaven and interfering with the kid's celestial joy.

Sometimes only a tearful song can link the mysteries of grief with hope.

~ *A time to mourn.* According to Ecclesiastes, "There is a time for everything, and a season for every activity under heaven: a time to weep and a time to laugh, a time to mourn and a time to dance."[10] This culture responds, "Yes, and the time to mourn will be Friday morning at 11:00 a.m. in the chapel of Heady Funeral Home."

In a preplanned/prepaid/pregrieved culture, we impatiently restrict openly expressed grief to funerals. Thomas Lynch, a funeral director and a respected commentator on funeral rituals, charged: "For the past couple generations, we've begun to think the major purpose of funerals is to be a warm, fuzzy event. So very often the dead are disposed of quickly and efficiently. We have farmed out the corporeal business of dealing with the dead to people like me, to professionals. And in its place put these tastefully upmarketed, well-organized, beautiful commemorative events that have really fine finger-food and plenty of mixed media and music and videos and, needless to say, uplifting, life-affirming talk. But the dead are not there. And in that sense, it's a little like going to a baptism without the baby there."[11]

One young funeral director invited a colleague of mine to develop an aftercare program. As she outlined plans for a six-week, ninety-minute-per-session program, the funeral director interrupted. "What I had in mind was two one-hour sessions. In my experience, that's really all they need." When my friend would not accommodate that timetable, the director found someone who would.

Dennis McGee, in an essay in *The Director,* the official publication of the National Funeral Directors Association, cited Martha Whitmore Hickman's contention that "to tell the story is a way of moving the grief along." "Moving along" sounds like something a waiter does when diners tie up a table. "Through service, experience and guidance, licensed funeral directors can share with families the importance of resolving grief and returning to normal living after the death of a loved one."[12]

Expecting funeral directors to help people resolve grief and return to normal living is outrageous. McGee also spun a new motivation for the funeral procession. "Historically, processing to a final resting place in a funeral cortege has ceremonially allowed mourners to divest in relationships with the deceased during life and begin to invest in new relationships with the deceased after death has taken place."[13] How can anyone divest relationships and invest in new ones during a ride to the cemetery?

Some people never experience an adequate ritual through which to voice their grief. They are offered a brief ritual moment designed to celebrate the life of the deceased rather than to lament. Throw in a few sentiments about how the deceased is now an angel watching over us, and we can still get to most of the agenda items for the day.

Some funerals are over — a poem, a point, and a prayer — before they have had a real chance to get started. Before grief had a chance to "get loose" and challenge our desire to be cool, calm, and collected in the presence of a corpse. Too many attend with a "Let's get this over with" mentality. In contemporary society we manage weight, anger, stress, and conflict — why not manage our grief too?

~ *The hurry-up generation.* In my memories of childhood I hear my grandmother's, "Hey, what's your big hurry?" I have wondered that in the parking lot after another rushed funeral or memorial service. I have driven away asking, "Why did I bother?" The funeral is not the end of mourning but a recognition of the collective impact of the loss. Ellen Goodman tackled societal impatience in a column aptly titled, "Mourning Gets the Bum's Rush": "I don't remember when the words first began to echo in the hollow aftermath of loss. But now it seems that every public or private death, every moment of mourning is followed by a call for 'healing,' a call for 'closure.' Last month, driving home in my car just 24 hours after three Kentucky students were shot to death in a school prayer meeting, I heard a Paducah minister talk about 'healing.' "

Before the teens had even been buried, a minister was declaring it was a time to begin the healing process, in Goodman's words, "as if there were an antibiotic to be applied at the first sign of pain among the survivors."[14] The minister might as well have waved a large checkered flag: "Mourners! Start your healing."

There are no start or finish lines in thorough grieving.

~ *Brief remembrances.* When President Warren G. Harding died at the Palace Hotel in San Francisco on August 2, 1923, First Lady Florence Harding requested that the Reverend James West offer a brief prayer in the presidential suite. Later she asked him to conduct a service "not to exceed fifteen minutes" before the presidential party left to return the president's remains to the White House.[15] Admittedly, President Harding had wanted a simple service, but fifteen minutes? At the brief service in the Capitol Rotunda, the First Lady showed what one observer called "iron determination," which attracted praise: "Mrs. Harding is the nerviest woman I ever saw. Maybe her lips quivered a bit yesterday when she leaned over the body of the President, but she did not give way. . . . Strong willed, I call it. That's the kind of stuff you find in good women anyway."[16]

What is the big hurry to escape grief's ability to upturn our sense of control and its ability to create chaos? Why are we in such a hurry to heal or recover or get on "to the next stage" in the words of one talk show psychologist?

What is our big hurry? Three days after September 11, President Bush stood in the National Cathedral and said to several thousand mourners, with millions watching on television, "We are in the middle hour of our grief."[17] Middle hour? Hardly. We were just at the beginning of the long trek through national and personal grief.

Impatience resurfaced on the eve of the tragedy's first anniversary. In an editorial for the *Kansas City Star* on September 11, 2002, I challenged that impatience: "I am afraid that many Americans, unacquainted with grief except as onlookers, are hoping that the first anniversary of September 11 will be a 'finale' to a fixation with grief."[18]

The controversy over plans for Ground Zero indicate the distrust — and disgust — of many people for thorough grief. Keith Sollenberger, in a letter to the editor of *USA Today,* said that there should be a "small memorial in tribute to those who were killed there," but "the bulk of the ground should be utilized like any other block of real estate in New York City." He insisted: "The memories of the dead and the pain we all feel do not need some massive memorial. We don't need an epic statue to remember this heinous act. The talk of 'hollowed ground' is nonsense. . . . Rather than allow the site to continue as a morbid scar on America, we should heal that scar and move on."[19]

Follow Sollenberger's logic and Gettysburg National Park could be turned into one incredible real estate development with condos, strip malls, and golf courses at a significant savings to taxpayers.

~ ***The Bible grants us permission to grieve.*** I wish a "Thus saith the Lord!" preceded "There is a time to mourn." I wish, from time to time, that grievers could hear those words proclaimed with the intensity of a loinclothed prophet like Amos or Micah! Sometimes we have to settle for a kind friend, one who has kept a grief, to remind us, "There is a time to mourn."

"There is a time to mourn" is one of the most liberating phrases in sacred literature. Those words gave

Jesus permission to keep his grief following the death of Lazarus, his friend. I think John's "Jesus wept"[20] could be translated as "Jesus *grieved.*" Jesus recognized and cooperated with grief. His crying led to the spin by some Jews: "See, how he loved him!" Then when Jesus came to his friend's tomb, he was "once more deeply moved."[21] Once more. Jesus did not just grieve once and for all.

If Jesus can weep and be deeply moved for a friend, you can weep and grieve and be deeply moved too. The American way of grieving interferes with any serious reflection on a loss. Ellen Goodman commented: "The American way of dealing with [grief] however has turned grieving into a set process with rules, stages, and of course guidelines. We have, in essence, tried to make a science of grief, to tuck messy emotions under neat clinical labels — like 'survivor guilt' or 'detachment.' "

As a result: "Sometimes, we confuse sadness with depression, replace comfort with Prozac. We expect, maybe insist upon an end to grief. Trauma, pain, detachment, acceptance in a year — time's up."[22]

Jimmie Holland, the chief of psychiatry at Sloan-Kettering, contends that "the expectation of healing" on some arbitrary timetable becomes "an added burden," as does the expectation that grief be tidy, at least in public. Dr. Holland's research led him to conclude, "Normal grief may often be an ongoing, lifelong process."[23] If only the president could have said that in the National Cathedral.

~ *Expedient grief is not a new expectation.* When Charlie Ross, press secretary for Harry Truman and his longtime friend, dropped dead in the White House in

December 1949, Truman could not hold a press conference for a week. (Truman had great difficulty even reading the official statement of condolence.) It just would not do to have a weepy president.

Truman planned a private funeral for his mother in 1947. His daughter recalled the days following her grandmother's death: "Two days after her funeral, Dad was back in the White House, still *grief stricken*."[24] In 2003, a Truman diary was discovered that shed light on the early days of his grief for his mother. His White House study became a safe place to mourn. Truman wrote, "I can shed tears [here] as I please — no one's looking."[25]

Years later, another White House occupant, George H. W. Bush turned down the family's request to do a eulogy for his close friend C. Fred Chambers, whom Bush called "my true, ever true, best friend" because he feared he would become emotional. He wrote the widow, "I hope I haven't let you down by not speaking in tribute to C. Fred."[26] Later, in his diary, he commented on saying no. "When something close and personal happens, I break up and I know it. I couldn't speak at Fred Chambers' funeral."[27]

Many Americans want national leaders and celebrities who model controlled grief. We want to emulate golfer Jack Nicklaus, who, when notified on the fourth hole that his mother had died, not only finished the round but played the next day in the PGA Tournament. "It will be a big day for both of us. . . . I'll have her in my thoughts," he predicted to reporters, who dutifully passed on the comments to sports fans. The next day he did tee off in a threesome with Tiger Woods and Vijay Singh. His mother "had one last wish — that her death not interfere with a big moment in her son's career." He played to respect her last wishes.[28]

Hours after their mother died, Michael and Ralf Schumacher raced in the San Marino Grand Prix. "She would have wanted to see us race today," Michael told reporters after he won the Formula One race.[29]

Conversely, Hollywood insiders were stunned when Goldie Hawn, following her mother's death in 1994, went into seclusion for three years. Goldie explored Indian and European spiritual philosophies, especially on the points of death and the meaning of life. "In a large sense," she recalled, "I turned a page when my mother passed on. I realized that all the things that I had been doing were simply not enough." There was more to life than stardom. Keeping the grief gave the actress time "to come to grips with death and what it was all about."[30]

~ *The rush to closure.* Anna Quindlen wrote, "The world loves closure, loves a thing that can, as they say, be gotten through." So we consider Goldie's grief keeping as a personality quirk; she always was a little zany. "It comes as a great surprise," Quindlen wrote from her own experience with grief, "to find that loss is forever, that two decades after the event there are those occasions when something in you cries out at the continual presence of an absence."[31]

Closure is expedited by the grief patrol, that cadre of therapists, psychologists, talk show hosts, and advice columnists who dispense answers to the universal question, "How long will this last?" *Dorland's Illustrated Medical Dictionary,* twenty-eighth edition, provides an acceptable answer to many professionals: "Mourning (mor' ning): the normal psychological processes that follow the loss of a loved one; grief is the accompanying emotional state. Four phases have been described: a short phase of numbness and denial, followed by a phase of yearning and protest marked by intense pining for the dead, followed by the phase of disorganization marked by pain and despair, ending in a phase of detachment and reorganization of love relationships that completes the work of mourning."[32]

Bill Worden, however, counters the prognosticators. The question has no answer; asking that question is like asking, "How high is up?"[33]

~ *Defining closure.* Dictionary definitions can be used like statistics to support any point of view. Consider entries under "closure" in *The Oxford English Dictionary*: "That which encloses, shuts in, or confines; a fence, wall, barrier, case, cover, setting, etc." and "the act of enclosing, shutting up, or confining."[34] The latter, especially, sums up what many people wish for grievers: to shut them up! They at least want to limit expressions of grief so it does not annoy others.

Witnessing thorough grief spoils any illusion of getting over it quickly. Americans are as anxious to contain grief as environmentalists are to contain an oil slick. That's why roadside memorials are controversial in many communities. In Kansas, the Department of Transportation removes them after six to eight weeks. In one Indiana community, a dispute erupted over a memorial site because neighbors charged that it was making it difficult to sell their houses.[35]

Only the persistent reader of the definition for closure finds: "a bringing to a conclusion; end, close." Ah, concluded grief. If you have not attained closure, at least show us some evidence that you are cooperating with the process. Or promise to try harder.

Bob Herbert wrote an essay in the *New York Times* in 2002 reflecting on grief, loss, and times past. In 1964, the bodies of Andrew Goodman, Michael Schwerner, and James Chaney, civil rights workers, were dug out of an earthen dam in Mississippi where they had been buried by Klansmen who killed them for helping African Americans register to vote. Herbert recounted: "I can't help also thinking about my friend Carolyn Goodman, who after all these years still grieves for the loss of her son, Andrew."[36] Mrs. Goodman would not come out favorably if analyzed by the criteria of *Dorland's* or *The Oxford English Dictionary* or Ecclesiasticus. Forty years, on the other hand, is not too long to grieve a son.

~ *The media's impatience with grief.* Just as many individuals discern significant news events from columnists, commentators, and pundits, many adults take their cues on grief from the media. Radio and television need to fill twenty-four hours of airtime, and newspapers and magazines need to fill their pages. Grief stories grab human interest, particularly if a celebrity is involved. Anguished-griever-following-a-casket photos appear daily in the newspapers. Sob photos demand our attention.

Two mornings after the *Columbia* disaster in February 2003, the *Kansas City Star* ran a front-page story about Lynne Salton, a local resident, whose sister, Astronaut Laurel Clark, died in the shuttle's disintegration during reentry. Lynne had been waiting at the Cape to celebrate her sister's landing. Under a large full-color picture of Salton holding her sister's official NASA photograph ran the caption: "Lynne Salton was still struggling to cope on Sunday after losing her big sister, astronaut Laurel Clark, in the shuttle Columbia disaster."[37]

Still struggling! The accident had happened only two days before! Your sister disintegrates in the skies over Texas and you're judged grief-incompetent because you are still struggling to cope two days later. I drafted a letter to the editor, which the *Star* published: "As a grief educator, I was stunned by the photo caption with the front-page article 'For Sister, a Long and Painful Wait, Then Heartache.' . . . How could anyone after only one or two days not be struggling to cope? All across Starland, readers and grief professionals acquainted with traumatic loss had to shake their heads in dismay: She will 'still' be struggling for a long time to come."[38]

Newspapers signal our cultural impatience with grieving. In Chicago in 2003, thirteen young adults died in the collapse of an apartment house porch during a summer night party. Tommy O'Connell, a survivor, was interviewed by reporters when he returned to the scene of the collapse. The *Chicago Tribune* reporter ended the story, "A day later he was still trying to come to grips with the fact that he survived when others didn't."[39] O'Connell will be still trying to come to grips with the collapse for years to come.

Violent deaths of the young are particularly "hot" news items. Ali Kemp, age nineteen, a lifeguard, was murdered as she closed a local swimming pool one evening. Eventually, a suspect was arrested and charged. The day of the arraignment, the *Star* ran a photo of the "still" grief-stricken father at the foot of his daughter's grave, freshly decorated with flowers. The caption read, "He visited his daughter's Mount Moriah grave Monday, something he does daily."[40] Daily! That convinced many readers that this father was dragging his feet. How could he get closure going to the cemetery every day?

~ **When a business tycoon grieves.** It is one thing when John Q. Average keeps a grief; it is another when a corporate tycoon does. Immediately after September 11, leaders in the business world asked, "When will the pain go away?" so the economy could get back to being the main thing. Reporters interviewed John Dasburg, then CEO of Burger King, who answered: "Never." Never?

Dasburg offered an alternative to the closure express lane. He learned by keeping the grief for his six-year-old daughter who was killed in a traffic accident. "No one can stand it, the pain is so intense. It has never gone away for me. You learn to live with it, you get accustomed to it, you accommodate it."[41]

After Meredith was killed, Dasburg made some corporate executives uncomfortable when he returned her picture to his desk — beside the pictures of his two living children. "I don't want to deny her memory. To say that I have two children is denying that she was here for six years."

Moreover Dasburg schedules a visit to her grave "whenever he is in Washington on business," although some colleagues consider the visits a sign of weakness.

~ **Grief marks us.** Grief leaves its mark. Grief significantly influenced Sherwin Nuland, a medical ethicist at Yale Medical School and author of the bestseller *How We Die*. His mother's illness and death (when he was eight) influenced his decision to study medicine. "All that I have become and much that I have not become, I trace directly or indirectly to her death."[42]

34

His father's death influenced how Nuland has lived his life. *Lost in America: A Journey with My Father* opens with Nuland and his own son standing in a cemetery, on one of his yearly visits. "Drew and I were standing before the grave of my father, now dead some forty years and yet in some ways more commanding and more needful than he had been during his life.... My father's power and the weakness that nurtured it have accompanied me all the days of my life. I have struggled to be the un-him — to be the opposite of what he was — and in the struggling I have faltered and fallen many times. His lingering power over me has been the source of much of my weakness."[43]

A National Book Award winner and eminent American physician, Nuland stunned readers: "I am writing this book to help me come to terms with my father. I am writing this book to finally make peace with him, and perhaps with myself."[44] Nuland kept his grief.

In the legend of Jacob and Esau, Jacob prepared to meet the twin brother he had swindled years before. Realizing that he might die at Esau's hand, Jacob wrestled with an assailant until daybreak. Neither could gain a submission from the other, until his opponent, wrenching Jacob's hip out of socket, demanded, "Let me go, for it is daybreak."

"I will not let you go," Jacob growled, "unless you bless me."[45]

The angel demanded, "What is your name?" Jacob answered, "Jacob."

"Your name will no longer be Jacob, but Israel," the wrestler explained, "because you have wrestled with God and with men and have overcome." With that, he blessed Jacob. Nevertheless, Jacob limped from

35

that place of blessing marked. He never walked normally again.

Some of life's most profound lessons are learned only through wrestling with grief. And limping into a changed future. God blesses those who give grief space and time.

Sherwin Nuland wrote about the influence of that cemetery visit on his son: "Though he never knew any of those with whose memories we come to commune — my father, my mother, Aunt Rose, and a baby brother who died before I was born — they have made their mark on him just as surely as though he had grown up among them in that small Bronx apartment of such emotional turbulence. But none of them has affected his life more than my father."

When we fast-track grief with a goal of leapfrogging the loss, we suggest to those we love that in due course we will forget them too. In a disposable culture, deep in our spirits, we suspect that we are replaceable and forgettable.

Reflections on loss. Death does not have to be the final line of a relationship's résumé. John Claypool's daughter died when he was the senior minister of the Crescent Hill Baptist Church in Louisville, Kentucky. Although in his years of ministry he had accompanied many grieving individuals and families, he wrote, "It was not until part of my own flesh and blood — my eight-year-old daughter, Laura Lue — was diagnosed with acute leukemia that 'my time came' and I was thrust inside the trauma of living with and through the mystery of dying" and grieving.[46] Out of his reflections, he wrote *Tracks of a Fellow Struggler,* which has been a source of comfort to millions. Twenty-five years after Laura Lue died, he revisited his grief in *Mending the*

Heart: "It is said that we human beings do not learn from experience itself but from our creative reflections on the experience. We do not have the power to go back and undo or redo the past, but we do have the ability to 'reperceive' the past and decide what meaning we will assign to those events for the present and the future."[47]

One sleepless night, John Claypool came to an insight that led him to keep his grief: "I realized at that moment a choice stood before me. I could spend the rest of my life in anger and resentment that she had lived so short a time and so much of her promise had been cut short, or I could spent the rest of my life in gratitude that she had ever lived at all and that I had the wonder of those grace-filled years."[48] Claypool chose the latter and used his experience as a blessing to help other grievers.

The goal in keeping a grief is not to be frozen into a time warp, a happy pre-grief era. The goal is to live in a grief-shaped present. Psychologist William Worden, after years of working with grievers, observed, "One benchmark" of growth is "when a person is able to think of the grief without pain." There will always be a tint of sadness, but it will lack "the wrenching quality it previously had."[49]

A grief keeper remains open, in Claypool's experience, to the creativity of God, who can "give us new things that will bring meaning and joy into our lives."[50]

~ **Stand at my grave and wail!** Only in a grief-deficient society would individuals want the poem "Do Not Stand at My Grave and Weep" read at funerals.

> Do not stand at my grave and weep.
> I am not there, I do not sleep. . . .

Abigail van Buren reported that the poem was one of the most frequently requested poems in the history of her syndicated column.[51] The poem's subtle message is: "Do not stand at my grave and grieve."

A better message would be, "Stand at my grave and keep the grief."

On the long journey to a far place, give yourself permission still to grieve as long as you need.

You Must Make Room
to Keep Your Grief

He that lacks time to mourn lacks time to mend.

— Henry Taylor[1]

The ladies stood in the cemetery. Both had been here before, one to bury a husband, the other to bury a child. Now the one was here to bury a child, the other a husband. They listened intermittently to the familiar words of the ritual and to the offered words of comfort — comfort that missed the mark. People were trying to be kind. "Count your blessings," the widows were repeatedly reminded. Neither would ever have to worry about money, even though it was the days before Social Security and the widespread popularity of life insurance and a husband's death often meant dire financial consequences. Nevertheless, the good life, as they had experienced it and expected it, was over for them.

Another time at a different cemetery, a dazed man stood at two graves in a February winter wind. Life had brutally ambushed him. Already political colleagues were lamenting that his future, perhaps his life, had collapsed: "He will never survive this. This would be too much for any man!" The trajectory that would have led the young politician to the seats of power in New York had been derailed by one of life's harshest but common realities: the untimely death of a wife during or following childbirth. Who could have imagined that his wife and his mother would die on the same day? On Valentine's Day? Hours after the deaths in 1884, to the sounds of a newborn daughter crying, the widower scrawled a large X in his journal and these words: "The light has gone out in my life."

Now as the minister closed the burial ritual, it was time to leave the dead. Some looked away as the politician was led away like a child. That night, he wrote, "For joy, or sorrow, my life has now been lived out,"[2] a heavy conclusion for a twenty-six-year old.

Minnie Taylor, pregnant at age fifty, a scandalous age for childbearing in her rural Texas community of Karnack, had fallen down a stairway in her home. Now Minnie, dying in a small hospital in Marshall, Texas, wanted to see her six-year-old daughter, Claudia. So the child's nurse, Alice Tittle, brought her to Minnie.

"Oh," Minnie groaned, "my poor little girl, her face is dirty." She asked for a cloth, washed the child's face, and then fell back in the bed crying, "Nobody at home to care for you. . . . Poor child." Alice took the girl out of the room, and Minnie died soon after.[3]

It was thought best that the child not attend the funeral. Days later, the minister who had conducted the funeral dropped by the home but committed a serious faux pas by suggesting to the grief-stricken husband that Minnie was better off in heaven than on earth. The father angrily confronted the minister.

"Preacher, how could you say such a thing? Who is going to take care of that little girl?" Claudia, who had never seen her father angry, made a decision that she must never make her father angry. She would always be

a "good" girl. Minnie died during the cotton harv
busy time of the year. Her father kept Claudia with
at his general store and cotton gin. Every night he made
a pallet for her on the floor in a storage room.

"Daddy," the inquisitive girl asked one night, "what
are those long boxes?" pointing to caskets that he sold.
Her father fumbled for an explanation.

"Dry goods, honey, just dry goods."

One biographer observed: "It's difficult to imagine
that Taylor would have been so insensitive to his daughter's feelings that he would have made a bed for her
near a coffin in the first few weeks after her mother's
death. Yet that is what he did. As a matter of sur-
vival, she learned early on to keep her emotions buried,
symbolically locked in a coffin in her soul."[4]

When school was out for the summer, Claudia's father
put her in a new dress, wrote on a cardboard sign "De-
liver this child to John Will Pattillo," and tied it around
her neck. Then he put her on a train for Alabama.
Although she spent the summer with her mother's relatives, the cousins were given strict instructions not to
say anything to upset Claudia. So this six-year-old had
to grieve alone in her mind.[5] At least Claudia knew her
mother was dead. Her two brothers, in boarding school,
would not be told for almost a year.

It seemed odd to be so dressed up in the middle of
the week in her best church dress but, in those days,
people dressed up for funerals. Life for blacks had never
been easy in segregated Birmingham, and it would be
years before anyone knew that the bombing of the Sixteenth Avenue Baptist Church that September Sunday

41

four children in Sunday school died,
ng point in the battle for racial equality.
ıg her parents' hands, the child walked
of the church for the funeral of her
friend, Denise McNair, killed in the
ьᴏɪɪɪᴠɪɪɪɣ. ᴏɪᴄ would never forget the stirring sermon preached by Martin Luther King Jr. Birmingham, the girl concluded, was not a safe place for a black child.

The young couple shivered in the January wind. They had traveled by train to Denver, her family's home, to bury their three-year-old son. His exuberance had been the delight of their lives and of the soldiers under his father's command at Fort Meade, Maryland. The little tyke had been looking forward to Christmas, especially after the tree went up in the living room.

Nothing at West Point had prepared this soldier for standing at his child's grave. How do you bury a child days after Christmas? The long train ride back from Denver did little to diminish the deep anguish raging in his heart. Already they had been told words that they would hear repeatedly that they were "still young" and "could have another child," but that sounded hollow to the couple who had loved Ikky.

~ *Predicting a future.* Had get-the-story-at-all-costs investigative reporters been around in those days they would have captured the agony in the faces, voices, postures, and lives of these grievers. No reporter would have sensed any hint of future greatness nor predicted that four of these grievers would live in the White House, another would work in the White House, one would establish a college, and one would build what would become a California tourist attraction.

While in those days no one would have expected them to get over their grief in thirty, sixty, or even ninety days, their grief would be the subject of comment in their families and social circles and, later, by biographers and historians. Each would keep their grief in a unique manner. But keep the grief they would. Their losses became defining influences in their lives.

None of these grievers were told, "You need to see someone" or sought professional help. None were given medications to dull the ache. None, at least according to my research, read bereavement books. None joined grief support groups.

Each, however, had a subterranean emotional stream flowing through their lives, surfacing at times, but always held in check lest it draw scrutiny, comment, or censure.

In time, these grievers would step forward to dance with destiny, just as they had danced with death. Each would gain recognition that they wished their loved ones could have seen, experienced, and shared.

Who were they? The two widowed mothers, Louise Newcomb and Sarah Winchester, kept their grief differently. In a séance, Sarah "discovered" a reason for the untimely deaths of her infant daughter, Anne, in 1866 and her husband, William, in 1881. They died, according to the medium, because of all the blood of Native Americans and Civil War soldiers killed by William's Winchester rifles. Mrs. Winchester was told that she could appease the spirits by moving west and building a great house. However, she would die the moment construction stopped. Sarah moved to San Jose, California, and began building. For thirty-eight years, crews of construction workers and craftsmen worked around the clock, seven days a week, 365 days a year. Sarah conducted séances every night to gain the plans for the next day. Some days the workers built, other days they tore down. At one point, the house had over seven hundred rooms, splendid Tiffany glass, a pipe organ, and a ballroom. Intensely private, she turned away the curious, including Theodore Roosevelt — who was insulted when told that he had to use the servant's entrance! Sarah spent some $5.5 million (an estimated $20 million in today's currency) on the house before she died on September 5, 1922. When her safe was opened, executors expected to find money. Instead, in a small box they found a lock of Annie's hair and the child's obituary from a Boston paper.[6]

Louise Newcomb, her contemporary, kept her grief for her husband, Warren, who died in 1866, and for her firstborn son. Following Mr. Newcomb's death she lavished her attention on her daughter, Sophie, until the girl contracted diphtheria and died four years later. Friends feared for Mrs. Newcomb's sanity. Although she made some initial financial gifts to memorialize her adolescent daughter, she wanted a more substantial memorial. At the suggestion of a friend, Mrs. Newcomb donated $100,000 — a sizeable sum in those days — to establish the Sophie Newcomb Memorial College. The nation's first coordinate college, this was a women's college affiliated with a men's college but with independent faculty, buildings, and financing. Over the years, Mrs. Newcomb gave more than $1 million and left her entire estate of some $2.5 million to the college, which eventually merged with Tulane University. Thousands of Southern women became first-generation college graduates through Mrs. Newcomb's generosity.[7]

What might the impact of the Winchester money have been if it had been invested in a philanthropic institution? Certainly, Winchester's money provided an exceptional standard of living for the families of Mrs. Winchester's laborers and craftsmen; they were paid three times the going wages in that area to buy their silence and maintain her privacy. Yet, ultimately, Winchester's legacy has became a tourist attraction — a living monument to poorly kept grief.

Theodore Roosevelt, who lost both his mother and wife on Valentine's Day in 1884, spent his life in the political arena vigorously limiting the claims of that grief. Like many men, he rebuilt his life with a new wife, Edith, and with more children (four sons and a daughter). Daughter Alice, named for her mother, remained on the margins of the new family and would never hear Roosevelt speak of her mother. In fact, he made no mention of his first wife in his autobiography. Biographer H. W. Brands concluded: "At some level he probably blamed baby Alice for her mother's death. Consciously, of course, he would have resisted any such bald formulation: Alice's death had been bad luck and perhaps God's will but not little Alice's fault. Yet at a deep emotional level he understood that if not for the baby, the mother wouldn't have died."[8]

It might have been better for everyone had the original plan — that baby Alice be reared by her paternal Aunt Bam — been followed. Although, in that era, it was common for second brides to deal with the ghosts of a first wife, this willful child would be an ongoing souvenir of a significant loss. As a child, an adolescent, and a young woman, Alice sought her father's approval and inclusion in his silenced grief. If anyone perfected "moving on" behaviors, it was Theodore Roosevelt. He had spent too much time defeating the forces of "weakness" in his life to give grief space.

The young girl with the dirty face grew up to become Lady Bird and married Lyndon Baines Johnson. I think that losing a parent at age five made her sensitive to six-year-old Caroline Kennedy's grief and influenced the decision to give Mrs. Kennedy time when leaving the White House.

The child in Birmingham, Condoleezza Rice, became provost of Stanford University and National Security Advisor for President George W. Bush. At the 2002 Stanford commencement, she reflected on the bombing's lifelong influence: "Although I didn't see [the blast], I heard it a few blocks away. And it is a sound that I can still hear today. . . . Those memories of the Birmingham bombings have flooded back to me since September 11. And, as I watched the conviction of the last conspirator in the church bombing last month, I realized now that it is an experience that I have overcome but will never forget."[9]

The couple in Denver, Dwight and Mamie Eisenhower, returned to life among young officers' families at Fort Meade. Mamie wrote relatives several days later, "Ike is up to his ears in work — which is good for him."[10] Their granddaughter later wrote of this period: "Though separated by an unbridgeable sorrow, in their wordless grief they clung tightly to one another. It was an act of love but also of bravery that ten months after Ikky's death Mamie became pregnant again."[11]

Eisenhower worked hard and rose through the ranks, gaining recognition as an Allied commander in World

War II. His bold direction of the D-Day invasion of Normandy earned him hero status in the public consciousness. His experience as a grieving father must certainly have influenced his meticulous planning for the invasion so as to limit the number of fathers who would lose sons in that military gamble. However, few who voted for him for president in 1952 or 1956 knew there had been a first child.

Throughout his military career and in the White House, Ike tended his grief. Often while playing golf with evangelist Billy Graham, away from listening ears in the Oval Office, he asked questions about eternal life. Could there really be reunion with Ikky and his mother? Graham assured him that there would be.

Mamie, however, kept her grief to herself. She insisted that she could not remember when the boy had died. Each year, on Ikky's birthday, when the general sent a dozen long-stemmed yellow roses — yellow being their son's favorite color — she always appeared surprised.

Mamie had difficulty keeping her grief — and watching her husband keep his grief — because she felt responsible for the death. She had grown up with maids; Ike had grown up in poverty on a Kansas farm. At Fort Meade, most of the officers' wives had maids, and she wanted a maid, too. Ike disagreed. The arguments grew more intense until, at the start of the holiday season in 1920, Mamie got her maid. Unfortunately, the maid had been exposed to scarlet fever and passed it to Ikky. Then meningitis set in. Doud Dwight — nicknamed Ikky because of his smelly diapers — died in Eisenhower's arms at Johns Hopkins on January 2, 1921. As an elderly man Eisenhower told historian Stephen Ambrose, "This was the greatest disappointment and disaster of my life, the one I have never been able to forget completely."[12]

Not until days before her death in 1979 did Mamie disclose her assumption that she had been responsible for the boy's death because she had wanted and hired the maid. All those years she had nursed that self-indictment. How might life, even in the White House, have been different if she had forgiven herself?[13]

~ **Keep your grief.** One does not have to be wealthy or famous to keep one's grief. It is simply a decision, not unlike the one a grieving Ebenezer Scrooge made, "I will keep [grief] in my heart." Actually, it may be a series of choices reaffirming that original decision and an unwillingness to give in to the subtle pressures from family, friends, and colleagues to suppress the grief and move on.

Contemporary society has a phenomenal desire to confiscate grief. Forget the notion that anything worth doing is worth doing well. To many minds, the only "good" grief is an expedited, efficient grief. Anyone perceived to be clinging to grief is branded a problem griever.

Those who ask, "How are you doing?" rather than, "How are you grieving?" want to hear some variation of, "Fine. It was tough at first, but we're doing much better now. Thank you for asking." Most people, eavesdropping on another's grief, don't want any hints that the grief may be long lasting, let alone a permanent component in a personal narrative like Eisenhower's or Winchester's. We want "grief recovery." Grief, however, is experienced, not recovered from, in the way that the economy recovers after a slowdown or a patient recovers after a serious illness.

Grief recovery is the ultimate embedded oxymoron in our society. Few question it. Many brutally indict themselves for being unable to "recover."

~ *Finding the courage to make room for your grief.* It takes courage to make room for one's grief, to go against the cultural wisdom that prizes minimized, brief grief. Males, particularly, are commonly counseled in other venues, "Dust yourself off and get back in the game!" In hushed parlors in funeral homes one can hear, "Best not dwell on it" or "Stay busy!" or other move-on messages communicated subtly.

Theodore Roosevelt stunned colleagues in the New York Assembly by returning and throwing himself into his work. "I think I should go mad if I were not employed," he explained. Two months later, in a political coup at the New York Republican Convention, he was elected a nonaligned independent delegate to the 1884 Republican National Convention.[14]

The corollary to "Stay busy!" for parents who lose a baby is "Have another baby as soon as possible." I silently groaned during a conversation with a couple who had recently lost a baby. Rather than focus on their grief, they focused their attention on getting pregnant again.

Martin and Katherine Luther, following the death of eight-month-old Elizabeth in 1528, devoted themselves to Magdalene, conceived soon after Elizabeth's death, because they "interpreted her birth as a consolation for the death of the little girl taken from them so quickly."[15]

So common was the advice to have another child right away that many males ended up widowers by following it. Martha Jefferson's final illness followed the birth of Lucy Elizabeth on May 8, 1782 — this baby named for the daughter who had been born eighteen months before and who had lived for only twenty weeks. Historian Jack McLaughlin assessed Martha's death: "Her death was ultimately caused, not by Martha's weakness or will or lack of determination to survive, but by the pregnancies resulting from the sexual demands of her husband." Thomas Jefferson "could not help but face this conclusion and hold himself responsible for his wife's death."[16]

We replace what we cannot fix. Many Americans believe grief to be just another problem to be solved or gotten over, another character-building circumstance to be challenged, another trial to deepen one's faith.

~ *Look for others to share your grief.* Many people are impatient with any honest expression of grief. "Mourning is fundamentally an intersubjective process," explained George Hagman, "and many problems arising from bereavement are due to the failure of other survivors to engage with the bereaved person in mourning together."[17]

In the absence of strong family or friend support, many seek out support groups. Unfortunately, some hope that the right group — or the right group leader — can "fix" them or that participation will accelerate their recovery from grief. However, there is no microwave equivalent for grief. There is no early release program. Grief ticks to a totally alien measurement of time.

Freud believed that grief was something of a paradox. In one sense, while mourning could be "completed," in a real sense, grieving is never completed. He wrote a friend, Ludwig Binswanger, whose son had died: "We find a place for what we lose. Although we know that after such a loss the acute stage of mourning will subside, we also know that we shall remain inconsolable and will never find a substitute. No matter what may fill the gap, even if it be filled completely, it nevertheless remains something else."[18]

The culture is obsessed with an abstract reality called "normal." People obsess over getting back to normal, meaning some predeath normal. The well-meaning often comfort, "Why, you'll be back to normal in no time at all." "Back to normal" has an appealing ring to it. Who wants to live with sorrow?

The only Normal I know is a university town in Illinois. If you want "normal," fly to Chicago, rent a car, and head southwest on I-55. You will find Normal.

No one gets normal back. Not unlike the first couple, Adam and Eve, who were prohibited from returning to Eden by the seraphim, we, too, are prevented from sneaking back into our old normal.

Grievers do, over time, with energy and strong support, construct a new normal. It doesn't get better, concluded my friend, Dennis, ten years following the death of his son. "It gets different."

~ *Give your grief time.* Our impatient culture seemingly encourages widowers to fast forward their grief with a new romantic interest. Some of television's best series have been devoted to that theme: *The Fugitive, Bonanza, The Rifleman, Family Affair,* and *Fury.* Each of Ben Cartwright's three sons had a different but dead mother. The Grim Reaper hung out at the Ponderosa.

I am taken by the grief of President Chester Arthur, a widower, who daily put fresh flowers in front of his wife Ellen's picture. Ellen Herndon Arthur had died in January 1880, twenty-one months before he assumed

51

the presidency following the death of James Garfield.[19] Wouldn't some psychologists have loved to get him into counseling?

~ **Some grief must be kept underground.** If the goal is to get over it or to move on, who wants to be labeled "grief challenged" or "grief impaired"? Too commonly, in contemporary Western culture, if individuals feel they must grieve, to avoid sanction or stigma they are expected to have the decency to do so out of sight. Grievers sometimes are not invited to social functions because the host fears the griever might spoil the gathering for others.

Some individuals are so good at disguising their grief that those closest to them may be unaware of their internal carnage, which may be a gentle stream or a ravaging flood. Think of those macho NASCAR drivers who sat stoically through Dale Earnhardt Sr.'s brief memorial and then, four days later, strapped themselves into race cars at North Carolina Speedway. Life and NASCAR go on. Sports reporter Skip Wood described their mood: "They came, they said, because that's what Dale would have wanted. They came, they said, because that's what they do — race. They came, they said, hoping to somehow find a measure of relief from the gut-wrenching emotions that had been tearing at them for the previous six days. Drivers said it. Owners said it. Crew members said it. Fans said it."[20]

Certainly they had the moment of silence at the Speedway for the seven-time Winston Cup winner. Former champion Darrell Waltrip asked fans to join hands while he prayed. His prayer was barely "Amened" before someone waved the checkered flag.

Dale Earnhardt Jr. explained his feelings and the feelings of fellow racers: "I just was really ready to get back to racing." Ironically, on the first lap, at nearly the same spot where his father died, between turns three and four, Dale Jr. smacked the wall.[21] Apparently, he was not ready to get back to the oval track after all.

Andy Petree, Earnhardt's crew chief, defended racing so soon after the death of a living legend. "It's hit a lot of people hard, and it's probably hit me especially hard. But I keep thinking about what he'd say if we didn't, that tone of voice. You know what I'm talking about — you've heard it a million times. He'd say, 'Hey, boy. What are you doing? Get out there and get in that car.' I mean, I'm not through crying yet, but this'll help."[22] This fast-forwarded grief was not lost on NASCAR fans.

~ *Disenfranchisement in communities of faith.* Unfortunately, in some faith communities, faith does not support keeping one's grief. Paul's guidance to the Thessalonians — "So that you do not grieve like... [those] who have no hope"[23] is frequently abbreviated and misquoted, "That you grieve not." So extensively is grief disenfranchised — if the deceased is thought to be "with God" — that noted New Testament scholar N. T. Wright felt the need to comment on the disenfranchisement among Christians in *The Resurrection of the Son of God.* "There is nothing unchristian about grief." It is, in fact, "a Christian phenomenon needing no apology."[24]

In the fifth century, Augustine declared that while a Christian could certainly mourn, even cry, sorrow "should not last too long."[25] In the sixteenth century, Martin Luther sternly rebuked his sixteen-year-old, Hans, following his sister's death, when Hans wanted to come home from boarding school to be with the family (he had come home for the funeral and then returned to school). Luther chided the headmaster, "As a result of the death of his sister and especially of the conversations with his mother, my son has become weak-hearted. But he must not give in to his sentiments, and he cannot come home, or he will never become a real man." Luther was more direct with Hans: "Do your best to master your tears like a man, and be careful not to give your mother pain again and not to make her anxious about you. . . . She wants you to master your sorrow and to study cheerfully and quietly."[26] Hans did not come home.

As President James Garfield died in 1881, Mrs. Lucretia Garfield, known for her Christian virtues, moaned, "Oh! Why am I made to suffer this cruel wrong?"[27] One newspaper account described the First Lady's stoic grief: "Mrs. Garfield bore the trying ordeal with great fortitude, and exhibited unprecedented courage. She gave way to no paroxysms of grief, and after death became evident, she quietly withdrew to her own room. There she sat, a heartbroken widow, full of grief, with too much Christian courage to exhibit it to those around her. She was, of course, laboring under a terrible strain, and despite her efforts, tears flowed from her eyes, and her lips became drawn in her noble attempt to bear the burden with which she had been afflicted."

Mollie Garfield, the daughter, however, was described as "naturally, greatly affected, and bursts of tears flowed from her eyes, notwithstanding her noble efforts to follow the example of her mother."[28]

~ *Minimalized sorrow.* Some Christians want minimal sorrow. Some want people to act like Lucretia Garfield and Hans Luther and Theodore Roosevelt, who can "take it."

In some churches, some people who keep their grief detect disapproval of their prolonged, unfinished grief. One griever serves on the staff of a megachurch. After his daughter's death, he felt highly visible to several thousand in the congregation as he sat to the right of the senior minister during services. Just months after his daughter's death, the senior minister and certain parishioners concluded that this man's sadness was distracting to the people in the pews. They wanted the old Reverend Herb back, not this unfamiliar man.

Late one Saturday night, the senior pastor called. He said, "Herb, can you put on a happy face for the people tomorrow? The people need to see you handling this victoriously." God forbid that congregants see anyone, especially clergy, in authentic grief in a worship service.

Herb soon detected a subtle shift in congregational support. Initially people asked, "Now, how are you doing?" and expected some type of synopsis. Soon, however, they asked, "How is your wife doing?" They would end the brief conversations — and the conversations became increasingly brief — with a pious, "We are praying for you" or "God bless you," which sounded patronizing to Herb. It became clear that congregants did not want to know how Herb was doing.

To say the least, Sundays took a toll on Herb's emotional and spiritual health. His church was not *mekom hanemkama* — a place of comfort or a safe place to grieve. Congregants did not want to be visually reminded every Sunday of a father's grief. Because if it happened to Herb, it could happen to them. Finally, Herb resigned and moved hundreds of miles away to serve a congregation that had never known his daughter!

Browsing a particular passage in *The New Interpreter's Study Bible,* used by thousands of ministers in sermon preparation, I was outraged by the commentator's notes on grief: "It is right to mourn the dead, but it is neither wise nor healthy to allow oneself to be consumed by grief. Even mourning should be done in moderation, for excessive grief does the deceased no good, and it can undermine the mourner's own health."[29]

I wonder if this scholar had ever danced with grief. Increasingly, many people find communities of faith hostile environments for authentic grief.

~ ***Make room in your life for grief.*** You cannot expect, these days, that others will actively support your grief. Not in your extended family, faith community, workplace, or social network. Visiting Old Town in Albuquerque, I stopped to read a large bright pink Certificate of Appropriateness on a building. Apparently, in Albuquerque, the city and the historical commission must approve any remodeling of structures in the historical district as appropriate according to historic preservation standards. In the fine print, I noticed the deadline by which the remodeling was to be completed. The sign brought back a story a young mother told me. Her physician informed her that grief, after six months, was inappropriate. Maybe we need Certificates for Appropriate Grief.

Keeping one's grief is an exacting, demanding psychological investment. It is easier to dodge or camouflage grief. Or limit grief to safe spaces and safe people.

Or pretend grief does not have power to grip our hearts at the most inconvenient times and have its way with us.

~ **Support may come from surprising resources.** Calvin Coolidge became president on August 3, 1923, following the death of Warren G. Harding. In July 1924, sixteen-year-old Calvin Jr., playing tennis on the White House courts, without socks, developed a blister on his toe. The toe became infected and he developed blood poisoning. Physicians had few ways to treat the condition. Calvin Jr. died at Johns Hopkins on July 7, 1924. The president groaned, "I don't know why such a great price was exacted for occupying the White House."

Several weeks later, early one morning, Colonel Edmund Starling, a presidential aide, arrived at the White House and found an eight-year-old boy standing at the front gate. When asked his business, the boy answered that he thought he might see the president. He had heard that the president got up early to take a walk. He wanted to tell him how sorry he was that his little boy had died.

Starling escorted the boy into the White House (in those days there was only minimum security) and into the Oval Office. The boy was overwhelmed and could not speak, so Starling conveyed his message. The grief-stricken Coolidge was deeply moved. Coolidge told his staff, "Whenever a boy wants to see me, always bring him. Never turn one away or make him wait."[30] Imagine the president of the United States being comforted by a young boy.

In those days, campaigns for the presidency began after Labor Day. Coolidge could not combine grief and campaign for reelection and did not make a single political speech. He relied on Charles Dawes, the vice presidential candidate, to do the campaigning, while he lost himself in sleep, often ten hours every night with long naps during the day.

Robert Gilbert, a political scientist who has researched presidential illness, concluded that Coolidge was clinically depressed. Calvin Jr.'s death reactivated unresolved griefs for his mother and sister who had died when the president was a boy. In those days, with limited media coverage of a president's personal life, his depression went unnoticed and, apparently, untreated.[31] Nine months later Coolidge was hammered by the death of his beloved father.

Scholars and historians have seized on Coolidge's statement, "When he [Calvin Jr.] went, the power and the glory of the Presidency went with him," as an explanation for his lackluster accomplishment as president. In an obsession with ranking presidents for effectiveness, however, his example of keeping his grief has been overlooked.

~ *Grieving in private.* Whenever grievers keep it to themselves, others are denied an awareness of their ongoing grief.

General Douglas MacArthur's mother, Pinky, had been the dominant influence on his life. When he went to West Point, his mother moved to the nearby Hotel Thayer to be close to her son. When he went to the Philippines as a military adviser, Pinky went with him. The general assigned her the hotel suite adjacent to him. A month after arriving in Manila, Mrs. MacArthur died and was temporarily interred, to be buried in Arlington National Cemetery on his next trip to the States. A devastated general locked her apartment for a year.

According to his aide, Dwight Eisenhower, the death "affected the General's spirit for many months."[32]

In 1937, MacArthur accompanied the president of the Philippines, Manuel Quezon, to the United States to round up support for training Filipino troops in light of Japanese military expansion in the Far East. Although Quezon expected MacArthur to accompany him to Europe, the general declined. His mother's casket had arrived in Washington, and he wanted to prepare for the burial. At Arlington, in the presence of a few friends, Mrs. MacArthur's casket was placed beside MacArthur's father. The general later reflected, "Our devoted comradeship of so many years came to an end."[33] In a macho military subculture, Douglas MacArthur kept his grief.

One man confessed, after a marriage of almost sixty years, "I don't know what I am supposed to do with my life without her." I suggested that he could do what MacArthur did: keep his grief.

On the long journey to a far place, make room to keep your grief.

You Have Permission
to Ignore the Stages of Grief

It is imperative to give ourselves permission to grieve in our own time and in our own way. Our culture's labels of what is weird and what is appropriate when grieving are hurtful and harmful.

—Barbara Roberts, *Death without Denial*[1]

Late on a July afternoon in 1981, as fifteen hundred people enjoyed the music and dancing in the lobby of Kansas City's Hyatt Hotel, two 120-foot walkways tore loose from their suspension rods and fell onto the packed dance floor. One hundred and fourteen people died, and more than two hundred were injured in one of the nation's worst structural failures. It was a horrible human tragedy. Yet in only seventy-five days, the hotel reopened. Life goes on.[2]

Twenty years later, there is no memorial on the site. Guests who walk through the lobby, attend meetings, or eat in one of the restaurants have no idea of the incident. I walk into that hotel and wonder, "Why is there no monument or marker here?"

Before writing this segment, I walked through a cemetery in my neighborhood. On a previous visit, I had been surprised by the many unused spaces. Surely the plots in this section had been sold a long time ago. Why were so few buried in this prime space? Then my foot struck something. I bent down and began pulling away clumps of overgrown grass and discovered a baby's grave marker. As I continued walking, I discovered more and more graves for infants that had become overgrown with grass over the decades. Did no family members visit? Had these dead children been forgotten?

Tonight, I spotted a bouquet of pink roses on one grave. Today would have been the child's thirty-fifth birthday. Someone remembered. Someone, in a "move-on" world, had kept their grief.

On Civil War monuments in town squares and on courthouse lawns across the South, I have read the phrase, or some variation, "Lest we forget." Today in my city, and in cities and communities across the country, the slogan could be "Lest we remember."

~ *The legacy of Kübler-Ross.* I walked into a friend's home minutes after her husband died. Her daughter directed me to the den, where a relative was delivering a talk about the stages of grief. I overheard: "Jane, there are five stages of grief. Number one is denial. I can look at you and see denial all over your face. You think Ed is still at the hospital. No! Ed is dead! You are denying it! You look at his chair and think that you will see him there in a few days, with a beer in one hand and a remote in the other. Jane, get it through your head: Ed is *not* coming home! Ever! He *is* dead!"

The speaker blitzed through anger, bargaining, depression, and acceptance. Then she said, "Don't you agree, Dr. Smith?" I did not want to dowse her enthusiastic recitation until she added, "I am certain that Dr. Smith will agree that you are in the first stage of grief." Both women looked at me.

"No, I do not agree."

61

"Do not agree? Everybody knows about the stages of grief!"

"The stages of grief is just a theory. We all grieve in our own way. . . . " I did not get to finish.

"Jane, I've got to go. I will check on you later." The woman left in what my mother called "a huff."

"You will have to overlook my sister," Jane apologized. "She means well."

"Jane, I don't want to go into the deficiencies of the stages of grief, but you will have to find *Jane's* way to grieve."

~ **Blessed are the grievers who have learned there are no stages of grief.** Some individuals think Moses carried the Ten Commandments and the Five Stages of Grief down from the Mount. That sounds outrageous unless you know that Elisabeth Kübler-Ross's stages applied to the dying — not the grieving. Somehow, perhaps because five stages are easy to remember, her theory was adopted as the way to move on after any loss. In dozens of continuing education programs, I have heard gasps when I dismissed the stages of grief as irrelevant. To some, that denial sounded like blasphemy. One minister moaned, "You have just destroyed everything I have shared with grievers during twenty-five years of ministry."

~ **Grieving in stages is a nice idea.** It's easy to wrap your mind around the stages of grief — denial, anger, bargaining, depression, and acceptance. Hear the theory once and you have the hang of it. The unspoken goal is this: grieve in an orderly way and someday, you too, will be a former griever.

Current practice is that the stages work like first grade, second grade, third grade, and so on. Master one stage and you advance to the next stage. It would be so much easier if grievers wore large numerals indicating their current stage. Individuals have explained in Grief Gatherings, "I am here because I did not do the anger 'stage'" or "I skipped the 'bargaining' stage." Many are convinced that had they completed a particular stage efficiently they would have been over their grief by now. So they come for some remedial anger or bargaining.

~ *Giving credit where credit is due.* Admittedly, Elisabeth Kübler-Ross gave Western culture a gift by talking openly about death, dying, and bereavement. At some point, a busy specialist decided that what Kübler-Ross had found among the dying — the dying persons she sampled — was true for all grievers. Like a brush fire, this idea leapt into new markets. Soon the stages of grief were on the tongues of almost every therapist with a shingle. At last, an expedient way to get 'em over grief because the first four all led to the real goal: acceptance! And acceptance equals over-it-ness. But an old wisdom says, "If it sounds too good to be true . . ."

Robert Neimeyer, with long clinical experience as a psychologist specializing in death, dying, and bereavement, rejected the notion that individuals experience any universal sequence of stages ending in recovery:

- I do not believe that the bereaved passively negotiate a train of psychological transitions forced upon them by external events.

- I cannot endorse the implication that a normative pattern of grieving can be prescriptive or diagnostic, and that deviations from such a course are to be considered "abnormal" or "pathological."

- I have doubts about the individualistic bias of traditional theories of bereavement, which tend to construe grief as an entirely private act, experienced outside the context of human relatedness.[3]

Neimeyer contended that a death "can validate or invalidate the assumptions on which we base our lives." Assumptions which, Neimeyer added, "provide us with a basic sense of order regarding our pasts, familiarity regarding our current relationships, and predictability regarding our futures."[4] To know me is to know my assumptions. To know my assumptions is to know my grief.

~ *Children are supposed to outlive their parents.* When parents bury their children, the psychological and spiritual turmoil can be grueling. Many mothers and fathers have been challenged in the AIDS epidemic by having to bury young adult sons. Edmund Hansen, following the death of his son, Dean, reexamined his assumptions through writing a book about his experience. "All my hurt," he later said, "leaked through my pen. It was my grieving for Dean."[5] Assumptions get in the way of interpreting and integrating reality.

~ *Wives are supposed to outlive their husbands.* When husbands bury their wives, particularly at an older age, their grief can be disabling. "We never once talked about this possibility," Clark told the group. "All of our finances and planning were based on the assumption that I would die first." Another widower told me, "I have no idea who I am without her." Neimeyer commented: "Forms of death that are discrepant with our core constructions (e.g., the suicide of a loved one or the chronic suffering and death of a spouse or child) can challenge the adequacy of our most cherished beliefs and taken-for-granted ways of living. In the latter case the degree of reconstruction of our patterns of interpreting, anticipating, and organizing our lives may be profound, and may never be fully accomplished from the death of our loved one until our own."[6] Some grievers carry a grief to their grave. How alien those words sound in a grief-impatient society.

~ *Institutions protect our children.* Pat Kutteles assumed the army would be a good place for her son, Barry Winchell. Imagine her shock on July 5, 1999, when notified that her son was dead. Not in the line of duty, but bludgeoned with a baseball bat as he slept in an army barracks at Fort Campbell, amid accusations that he was gay. The army, without consulting Pat, accepted a plea bargain from his two assailants at their court martial. The army assumed the matter — and this mother — would just go away. Imagine the commanding general's surprise when he went up for promotion to third star to discover opposition led by one grief-keeping mother from Kansas City![7]

~ *"One size fits all" does not apply to grief.* No one theory of grief applies to every griever. Rather grief is a personal process, Neimeyer argued, "idiosyncratic, intimate, and inextricable from our sense of who we are."[8] Grief is not poured into a mold to achieve uniformity. You may tell me that your mother died, and because my mother died, I may have some inkling of your experience. However, to understand your grief I must understand your relationship to your mother. Any theory of grief has to be flexible enough to accommodate the infinite variety of individual behaviors, feelings, meanings, and personal narratives.

According to Neimeyer, "Our personalities, outlooks, and dispositions are determined neither by our genes nor our environment, but by our own investment in those persons, places, projects and possessions in which we are bound by bonds of caring attachment."[9]

When people tell you that you should be over it by now or raise their eyebrows and snarl, "What? Still grieving!" before responding, wiggle your thumb and remind yourself of your right to grieve your way.

~ *Public and private rituals.* Following the death of Prince Albert, Queen Victoria developed an intense, some thought scandalous, attachment to commoner John Brown. They appreciated each other's companionship. Brown died in 1883, and on the first anniversary of his death she wrote in her journal, "I cannot cease lamenting."[10] Now the queen had to juggle two griefs. Hough, a biographer, suggested that her statement may equally have applied to Prince Albert. In many ways, the queen's relationship with Brown offered a distraction from the public obsessive grief for Albert.

Eighteen years later, Queen Victoria posthumously acknowledged Brown's claim on her emotions. Although the court knew of her grief rituals for Albert, few knew of her ritual act for Brown. In the dead queen's left hand, as per her instructions, Sir John Reid placed a photo of Brown and a locket of his hair, wrapped in paper tissue. Then he covered that hand with her daughter Alexandra's flowers.[11]

~ *Defining me now.* Who am I now? Who am I without my loved one? These are questions grievers ask. Some children want to know, "Am I still a big sister?" Many grievers have not known an adult identity other than that shared with a particular individual. One seventy-year-old widow said, "He's all I've ever known. We married the week after we graduated from high school." Parents have to renegotiate their family's identity with surviving children following the death of a daughter or son, particularly if the surviving siblings considered the deceased "the favorite" or a problem. Paul Newman had five surviving daughters, but he had to deal with the death, due to drug overdose, of his "difficult" child, Scott.[12]

Many individuals have to reidentify themselves following tragedies, particularly tragedies that trigger extensive media attention. One widow of a firefighter who died at Ground Zero told me that, although they had a good marriage, she did not want to spend her life known as his widow or as a September 11 widow.

Glacia Burnham's husband was killed in a firefight between Abu Sayyaf rebels and Philippine troops during a rescue raid in June 2002. After being held hostage for a year with her husband, she had to figure out what it meant to be free and a widow. In the evangelical Christian subculture, missionaries are regarded as heroes. This meant certain grief options were not open to her. "Some people want me to be depressed and morose — the poor, whimpering widow," she told an interviewer. "What good would that do?"[13] Others were not pleased with her statements that their missionary agency should have paid the ransom that the rebels demanded for her and her husband.

For some September 11 survivors, identity and support were linked to socially sanctioned relationships: husband, wife, daughter, son, spouse. Individuals who were not married to victims faced a crisis in support and compassion. Twenty-two individuals in gay or lesbian relationships had to deal not only with the reality that their partner was not coming home but that they initially had no legal standing for compensation and benevolence. The master of the federal Victims Compensation Fund ruled that any payment to a partner must have the approval of the biological family. Given the government's limitation of only one request for compensation per victim, one survivor, John Winter said, "I feel close to his family. But money can change things."[14]

~ *Grieving in the public eye.* Barbara Roberts had to balance grief following the death of her husband with her responsibilities as governor of Oregon. No longer could she turn to her husband, Frank, for advice. She had to define: Who am I without Frank as First Husband? Years after her husband's death, she reflected on her grief: "I am convinced, more than ever, that our culture has labeled as 'weird' some of the most wonderful, precious, and sensitive acts of grief. . . . We may choose to keep our secrets but we need not feel strange about choosing our path for grieving. Or we may decide to tell part of our secrets so that others may learn from them and may know they are not alone."[15]

Individuals who grieve unashamedly risk being labeled "crazy." If I had a dollar for every time a griever has exclaimed, "So, I am not crazy after all!" I could afford a villa on an island in the South Pacific. Grief is in the eye of the beholder.

Consider this widow's ritual — after thirty-five years of marriage: "She continued to live in their Paris house. . . . She kept her husband's things exactly as he had left them, down to the clothes in their cupboards and the cigars in their boxes, and every evening would go to his room, still adorned with numerous pictures of herself, and whisper, 'Good night, David.'"[16]

The widow did this for three-and-a-half years until her own death. How would you assess her mental and emotional state?

- Needs to see someone?

- Needs to take something?

- Needs to join a support group?

Would it make a difference in your response if you knew that "David" had been King Edward VIII of England, before his abdication to marry this woman? When I tell this story of the duchess of Windsor's grief, I get one of two responses: "Wow! How wonderful!" or "How pathetic!"

Grief, according to philosopher Tom Attig, is a journey that prepares us, over time, to love in new ways and to live in new ways in the active absence of the loved one. We do not rip threads out of an emotional tapestry and throw them away. Rather, "we reweave the threads of our lives, creating new integrated patterns."[17] For some, the reweaving can be dramatic. Some grievers blossom while others become emotional hermits.

Attig is clear: "We change, as do our enduring connections with those who have died, with our families, with friends, with the larger community, with God, and even with our life's work."[18]

Sadly, there are some who must also grieve for relationships and friendships that wither following the loss. Sometimes the deceased was the glue that held a friendship together.

~ *Grief in the express lane.* Many people do not want a meandering, unfolding path to recovery. Oh no! Many grievers want to grieve in the express lane—some even simultaneously auditioning a new romantic relationship. "Gotta get there!"—meaning over it, as quickly as possible—is the goal.

Life has a way, however, of blocking the express lane with road treads or bumps that warn a lane is ending. Simple things, like folding laundry, remind and may require adjustment in routines. One widower said, "I had always folded towels in half until I met my partner, who insisted that I fold them in thirds. I miss him particularity whenever I do laundry. Sometimes I don't even fold them." In remembering, grievers find new ways to love in absentia.

~ *An alternative to the stages of grief.* J. William Worden, in his classic text, *Grief Counseling and Grief Therapy,* offers four tasks that provide a nurturing, griever-friendly framework for the work of grief—and grief is work! The tasks are:

- to accept the reality of the loss;
- to work through *to* the pain of the loss;
- to adjust to environments in which the person/object is missing;
- to "relocate" and memorialize the loved one.[19]

~ *Accepting the reality of the loss.* Some individuals will not accept their loss. An outcry arose when Rudy Giuliani ordered that the rescue operations at Ground Zero become a recovery (of bodies) mission. Grievers had to accept, however painful, the reality of their loss. To dodge the pain, some people turn bedrooms into shrines or museums, and mummify their grief. C. S. Lewis warned about the temptation "to prove to ourselves that we are lovers on the grand scale, tragic heroes; not just ordinary privates in the huge army of the bereaved, slogging along and making the best of a bad job."[20]

For forty years following Prince Albert's death, Queen Victoria of England had his clothes laid out daily. Forty years! One reason for this behavior may have been that she was not allowed to touch Albert's corpse or attend his funeral.

Somewhere, as you read this, a parent is vigorously denying the death of a child by maintaining the room exactly as a son or daughter left it. Some families create shrines complete with urn, candles, photos, flowers, and personal effects. That decision can become a source of tension between spouses, children, grandparents, and concerned others who consider this decision proof of pathological grief. For others, this is a transitional way to get used to the reality.

Some may not keep rooms intact, but keep clothes, automobiles, or objects, or a desk or workspace exactly as the deceased left it. Other families have immediately turned a bedroom or playroom into a den or office space.

Queen Elizabeth II, in an attempt to control her world following the death of Princess Diana, decided that the entire royal family would attend church on Sunday morning. She ordered that no mention of the death be made in the prayers for the royal family or in the homily. As a result, the sermon was sprinkled with jokes from Scottish comedian Billy Connelley. After the prayers, Prince Harry leaned over and whispered to his father,

"Are you sure Mum is dead?" The Reverend Robert Sloan explained that the tragedy was ignored "to protect the boys."[21] Hardly. It was to protect the adults from a corpse!

~ *Direct disposal.* The growing practice of "direct disposal" interferes with accepting the reality of loss. Immediately after death, an individual's body is cremated. Thomas Lynch charged: "A quick and private disposal of the dead removes the sense of emergency and immediacy from a death in the family. No need, as W. H. Auden wrote, to: 'Stop all the clocks, cut off the telephone.' There is no bother with coffins at all. The dead are secreted off to the crematory or grave while the living go about their business."[22]

There is something to be said for viewing a corpse. In too many cases, someone, acting on behalf of the family, has decided that family members and friends should not see the body — especially after violent deaths resulting in significant disfigurement. The practice gained acceptance during the Vietnam War when dead soldiers returned in body bags with the government's assurance, "Trust us. This is your son."

Many funeral directors now offer to drape the body and expose a portion that is not disfigured to accommodate a moment with the actual deceased. "I would recognize these feet anywhere," one mother said, stroking her sixteen-year-old's feet.

Some accept the reality of their loss through a series of confrontations with a corpse. Ralph Abernathy, the trusted lieutenant of Martin Luther King, was with King when he was shot on the balcony of a Memphis motel in 1968. At the hospital emergency room, in front of the doctors and nurses, Abernathy took his friend in his arms as he died. "The breaths came farther and farther apart. Then, a pause came that lengthened until I knew it would never end."[23]

After notifying his aides, Abernathy left to meet Coretta Scott King at the airport. When he learned that Mrs. King would not come until the next day, Abernathy instructed the driver, Solomon Jones, "Take me where my friend is." They returned to the hospital where Abernathy was informed, "We need someone to officially identify the body." Abernathy described this encounter with his friend's corpse. "[I] saw on a metal table, a body covered with a piece of brown paper that reminded me of the wrapping paper butchers used in country stores. Protruding from underneath were two feet, and on one of the toes a tag was tied. The young man lifted the piece of paper, and I saw him again, somehow more dead than he had seemed when I left him in the hospital room. I nodded. 'This is the body of Martin Luther King Jr.,' I said."

That was an encounter with the reality of death. When the attendant asked Abernathy to authorize a postmortem, after calling Mrs. King, Abernathy signed the paperwork.

A third encounter took place at 3:00 a.m., when Abernathy went to the funeral home where Dr. King's body had been transferred. When he asked to see the body, the mortician tried to talk him out of it. Finally, yielding to Abernathy's determination, the director warned Abernathy, "We have just received the remains from the hospital and haven't had a chance to do our own work."[24]

Abernathy recalled: "I had never before viewed a corpse that had undergone an autopsy, and I never want to see another. The sight haunts me yet, though for some reason I had to see it, would never have felt I'd satisfied my obligation to Martin if I hadn't seen his body at that moment. . . . I stared for an instant, a mute witness to the final dehumanization of Martin Luther King Jr., his transformation from person to thing. I knew in that moment that I could leave this body now, leave it forever, because it no longer belonged to my friend. I was ready for burial."[25]

Later Abernathy returned to approve the embalmers' work. The casketed corpse would be the memory he kept rather than the body lying in blood on the motel balcony, in the emergency room, on a morgue table, or on an embalming table.

~ *The viewing and wake.* Historically, the viewing, as it is termed in many parts of the country, was important to ensure community acceptance that the individual had died and had not been subject to foul play. Before coroners and medical examiners and embalming, the community needed assurance that the death had not been a homicide or suicide. Someone has defined the purpose of a wake as a time to make sure the dead are dead and that they stay dead.

Before funeral directors became established, preparing the body was the responsibility of family and friends. Often preparation took place in the residence, which drove home the reality of the death. In Judaism, although the corpse is not viewed, certain members of the Jewish community, the *chevera kiddish,* wash and dress the body. Increasingly, across the faith spectrum, individuals are asking for the privilege of washing and helping prepare or dress the body.

Given the significant number of individuals who die in hospitals and nursing homes, sometimes with limited recent contact with family and friends, and given the mobility in many families, individuals may have difficulty believing that a family member is dead until they view the corpse. It was not until I walked the corridor of Ratterman's Funeral Home, into the parlor, and viewed my mother's body that I was able to say, "My mother is dead."

~ *Sometimes the body cannot be recovered.* Lt. Denis Anderson, U.S. Navy pilot, had told his bride, Sue, that if anything happened to him he wanted to be buried in Arlington National Cemetery. Months later in January 1968, Anderson and eight crew members of the OP-2E *Neptune,* on a mission over Laos, crashed into the side of a mountain. Sue and other family members were repeatedly told that it was too dangerous to recover the bodies. Sue remarried in 1970. Thirty years passed.

Between 1993 and 2002, six joint U.S.-Laos body recovery missions worked the site, identifying and recovering remains. In May 2003, Lt. Anderson's remains were positively identified at military identification labs in Hawaii. When notified, Sue flew to Honolulu to accompany her first husband's remains to Washington for burial at Arlington. Sue called the discovery of Lt. Anderson's wedding ring, found at the crash scene, "an answer to prayer." The ring she had given him in 1966 confirmed the reality of his death.

Initial estimates set the cost of this recovery at more than $15 million. This demonstrates the commitment of Americans to recovering our dead and to providing an honorable burial. Thirty-five years after his death,

Sue Anderson Jenkins fulfilled her promise to Denis Anderson. He and his eight crew members were buried in Arlington National Cemetery. Not in a mass ceremony, but with each officer honored on separate days in separate rituals.[26]

~ *Working through to your pain.* Grievers must work through *to* the pain of their loss. Worden is frequently misquoted. He did not say "to work through the pain," which is preferable in a "Get over it!" culture. Americans are ingenious at attempting to dodge the pain of grieving.

Some people are never really given a chance to work through to their pain. The medical community views death as a failure. Some physicians believe grief is a problem to be solved pharmacologically rather than experienced. "I can give you something," offers the well-meaning-but-busy physician. Once upon a time, a family physician, who possibly knew the family well, would have offered sage comfort and counsel.

In managed care the average physician-patient interaction is eight minutes.[27] How can a woman married fifty-four years explain her grief to a physician in eight, or eighteen, minutes? Instead the physician reaches for a prescription pad or refers the patient to a therapist.

Pain has ways of fooling individuals. Some, in initial grief, run on adrenaline. "Gotta get through the funeral, settle the estate, then ... " Paul Newman, following the death of his son, reminded reporters, "We have a lot of anesthetics in today's society, a lot of things that dull our lives."[28] Newman experienced intense pain when his movie *Harry and Son,* influenced by his grief for son Scott, received disastrous reviews. Fearing that the movie would die at the box office, Newman blitzed the morning news shows and did numerous interviews with newspaper and magazine reporters. Whenever interviewers linked *Harry and Son* with Newman's grief, Newman answered: "You cannot fictionalize grief."[29]

~ ***Adjusting to environments where the person is missing.*** Bob Hope closed his USO shows crooning, "Thanks for the memories." Memories link individuals with places. The popular adage, "Out of sight, out of mind" fails in issues of loss. "I see her everywhere I look," one parent told me after his seven-year-old's death. Grievers must confront the particular absence in familiar, intimate settings or events or experiences. For some, it is an absence at a dining room table or a kitchen; for others, in a bed. "It's the long nights that get you," my widowed mother often told me.

The dead are remembered in familiar spaces: in dens and offices, bedrooms and bathrooms, basements and garages, churches and ball fields, classrooms and gymnasiums, malls and concert halls, gardens and parks. The dead are remembered — even if not acknowledged — at parties and open houses, weddings and graduations, receptions and reunions, annual meetings and committee meetings. Wherever we gather, wherever we celebrate, we have to make room for their absences.

Grievers feel the absence more significantly in certain locations. Harry Truman, as a senator and president, had always headed home to Missouri for the Christmas holidays until Christmas 1947. He could not emotionally face his mother's absence in her home in Grandview, so he invited the Truman clan to spend Christmas at the White House.

What was life at 1600 Pennsylvania Avenue like for Calvin and Grace Coolidge after Calvin Jr. died? What was it like to walk into the East Room, remembering that their son's wake was held there? Coolidge confessed to one Oval Office visitor, "When I look out that window, I always see my boy playing tennis on that court out there."[30] It is not surprising that he gained the nickname Silent Cal.

~ *Relocating and memorializing your loved one.* Worden, in previous editions of his text, used the phrase "to emotionally relocate the deceased and move on with life" as the fourth task of grieving. In 2002, he modified this task to be: "to relocate and memorialize the loved one" since the phrase "move on" had been misunderstood. Grievers must find "an appropriate place in their emotional life" for the deceased.[31] What, then, does the griever do with those memories? Worden enlisted V. D. Volkan's assessment: "A mourner never altogether forgets the dead person who was so highly valued in life and never totally withdraws his investment in his representation. We can never purge those who have been close to us from our own history except by psychic acts damaging to our own identity."[32]

Too many individuals grieve with the unwritten assumption that they have to purge their memories to be rid of the dead. Maybe you have seen movies where security technicians sweep a room for hidden recording devices and then declare the room clean. Many helpers think the goal of grieving is to have a blank memory.

~ *Purging frantically.* Florence Harding worked frantically during nights in the White House following her husband's death. The Oval Office, particularly Harding's desk and safe, had been thoroughly searched for letters or photos linking him sexually to Nan Britton and other women. It may have been August, but Mrs. Harding kept the fireplace in the family quarters blazing, burning letters and documents — anything that might be misconstrued. (Admittedly, Martha Washington, as a widow, had burned George's letters, too, but for different reasons.)[33] "She began to hand [Reedy Baldinger, an aide] papers. Often she came over to look at the burning papers and stir the ashes herself with a brass poker. Sometimes she didn't even trust Reddy, making sure some letters went directly from her hand into the fire. This went on for five nights, the Duchess thrusting into the flames other 'confidential and personal' papers that she had rummaged from the Oval Office during the day."[34]

Many of Harding's official and personal letters were destroyed. As time ran out, Mrs. Harding stuffed papers into ten-foot crates to sort through later, reminding Reedy, "Reedy, we must be loyal to Warren and preserve his memory."[35] Mrs. Harding wrote dozens of friends, asking them to return all original letters signed by the president, under the guise that she was going to amass a collection of Harding's papers for future researchers.[36]

After the burial in Marion, Ohio, every morning for six weeks she was driven to her husband's old office. As Florence rifled through the crates, she kept a pot-bellied stove blazing. Initially she had planned to return to Washington on November 1, 1923. She wrote a family friend, "I am sure it's going to take me much longer to go through them than I anticipated."[37]

Biographer Carl Sferrazza Anthony mused that it was not simply "a matter of a bereft widow trying to keep a few past incidents private. . . . [Mrs. Harding] did not

79

want the general public or press to know what she was doing."[38]

Admittedly, not every griever has as many secrets to hide as did Florence Harding. Yet many are influenced by the cultural admonition, "Speak no ill of the dead."

Distinctions between giving up and moving on can be fine ones. Honesty, to many, feels like betrayal, especially if there are children. Many of the young American widows of the Iraq War will raise children whose fathers died in Iraq. How do you keep alive a memory in a world that wants you to move on, especially after a war was won? *USA Today* surveyed several war widows and concluded, "They are struggling to move forward."[39] Perhaps "move forward" will replace "move on" as the new cliché for this generation.

Linda Goldman, who works with military widows, noted, that, for some, a baby is a joyful distraction from grief. "I think they really value that they have a part of their husband that will live on with them through these children. And that's a blessing, but also an ongoing memory of their husbands that they lost."[40]

One psychoanalyst, Elsa First, commented on war widows, "These deaths are the toughest on the young widows because they were good, young, hopeful families, and widows need a long time to grieve." (I was delighted to read that assessment.) Why? Because they are grieving not only "the loves they lost" but "the lives they planned."[41] Moreover, they are grieving in a postwar euphoric, "We kicked some Iraqi butts!"

In some cases, the grief is enhanced for these widows because, for some time, they made good copy for the media. However, as Shauna O'Day, age twenty, told reporters, "You kind of want your privacy back; you want your life back."[42]

~ *The role of professionals.* Many professionals believe the goal for the griever is to transfer emotional attachment from the deceased to a new relationship, which becomes the proof of the pudding of their recovery. Tony Walter, a British sociologist, will have none of this. "It is entirely up to the individual whether he or she chooses to go on and form new attachments, there being no clear evidence that forming new attachments is correlated with effective functioning."[43] S. R. Schuchter and Sidney Zistook theorized: "A survivor's readiness to enter new relationships depends not on 'giving up' the dead spouse but on finding a suitable place for the spouse in the psychological life of the bereaved — a place that is important but leaves room for others."[44]

~ *Creating a cherishable memory.* Denman Dewey suggested a task that complements Worden's tasks: creating a cherishable memory. The deceased still has a role, perhaps a valued role, in the survivor's biography; in fact, Tony Walter argues that the deceased and survivor continue to "share" narrative space.[45] In forming a cherishable memory, the bereaved weaves a lasting memory. In some cases that is easy. Others find that difficult due to abuse, estrangement, or betrayal. Imagine the task that Florence Harding faced. As the scandals broke, her memories were continuously bashed.

Grieving quilters once took fabric from shirts or from dresses to sew into a quilt design to honor someone's memory. Grievers can take memories and weave them in a new lasting memory. The Hawaiian word

81

humuhumu — fitting the pieces together — shares that sentiment. Grievers fit their pieces of memory together.

Some grievers keep reindicting "the son of a bitch" rather than acknowledging the whole person. Crafting a cherishable memory is demanding psychological work and requires time and, often, the assistance of a caring professional. No few sons and daughters have, in time, come to grant a measure of absolution, "She did the best she could."

Alexandra Mosca, attending both the visitation and burial of John Gotti, a Mafia boss, discovered that not everyone considered him just a mobster. "Whatever his deeds, Gotti had also been a husband, father, grandfather, brother, uncle and friend to many. And these people were all here to honor him. . . . In fact, the consensus of those attending was indignation that a Catholic had been denied a Mass of Christian Burial, no matter what sins he may have committed in life."[46]

In time, people generally reconcile the realities, indignities, and eccentricities of the deceased, creating a cherishable memory. To those who continue to snarl, "I hope he burns in hell," I wonder whether it is worth the emotional energy invested in keeping an uncherishable memory.

~ *Letting go of grudges.* While I do not believe in letting go of a grief, I do believe in, after reflection, letting go of grudges and ill-will that can shape our grief. That only happens when we abandon claim checks to justice.

The encounter happened over dinner. I had spoken at a church, and the minister had organized a small dinner with parishioners afterward. Over the course of a delightful meal, when the conversation turned to politics, I said something about Senator Gary Hart, then running for president.

"The Gary Hart that murdered my son?" one man demanded angrily.

"No, I am talking about Senator Gary Hart . . . "

"That's the same Gary Hart who murdered my son!"

"What?" I realized, in the heat of politics, people make strange allegations about politicians, but this was absurd. Conversations around the table stopped.

"There's no difference in what he did and holding a gun to my son's head and pulling the trigger. He worked for McGovern. My son died in Vietnam because of those two." An hour earlier I had spoken on forgiveness. Now his friends, used to these episodic tirades, embarrassed, wondered how I would respond. Some clearly hoped that I could disarm this father's anger.

I looked across the table at the father and took a breath. "I am sorry that your son died in Vietnam. But Senator Hart did not murder your son. He advocated policies with which you disagreed. Blaming Senator Hart will not bring back your son. And it will not bring you peace." Needless to say, no one ordered dessert.

While this wounded man has kept his grief for his son, the anger he has kept at a high pitch has alienated him from the friends and associates who really care for him. I am sorry, in Worden's words, that he has not found an appropriate place for his son. Sadly that father died with his anger intact. Few attended the funeral. The anger, not the death, ruined his life.

~ *Grief does not flow on any timetable.* Rushing individuals through their grief — not saying, "Slow down!" as we would to a child gobbling down a meal, not allowing grievers to keep their grief — we do violence to their personalities and to their futures. Charles Corr offers sound thinking: "No one has to [grieve] in any particular way. To insist that individuals must cope ... in what others regard as the 'right' or 'correct' way is simply to impose the additional burden of an external agenda upon vulnerable persons."[47]

Grieving is more than navigating a series of stages in order to arrive, "recovered," in a land called "normal." It is about giving grief a space in our lives, memories, and hopes.

On the long journey to a far place, give yourself permission to ignore the stages of grief.

You Have Permission
to Lament

Permission to grieve granted.
—Barbara Lazear Ascher,
Landscape without Gravity[1]

On August 22, 1914, in the third week of the fighting of what became World War I, General Ferdinand Foch learned of the death of his only son, Germain, a twenty-five-year-old infantryman. Many of the staff wondered how the elderly general would handle such devastating news. He asked to be left alone. Thirty minutes later, he emerged and said, "I can do nothing more for him. Perhaps I can still do something for France. Back to work."[2] Hours later he would learn that his son-in-law, Captain Charles Becourt, died in the same battle and had been buried in the same mass grave with Germain near the France-Belgium border.[3]

The war had to go on just as Harry Truman, after his mother died, had to grieve and fight on for his political life in the election in 1948, a tough campaign against Dixiecrat Strom Thurmond and Republican Thomas Dewey. I have read through boxes of condolence letters, cards, and telegrams that Truman received — many with the words, "I know what you feel...my mother died last year." Many writers encouraged the president to "buck up." After all, Truman had become famous for the sign on his desk: The Buck Stops Here! Lottie Healy Jackson admonished him, "I am sure she would want you to look bravely into the future and to be courageous."[4]

F. J. Bowman challenged the cultural notion that one should not grieve too dearly for the elderly. He also said, "But at any age, the loss of a mother is a special bereavement. To be cut off from the one who bore us, nourished us and taught us the first and deepest lessons of life, leaves us lonely in a way no other deprivation can."[5]

~ **Laments may make people uncomfortable.** The Olympic medals for the Athens summer games in 2004 had a new design. The Olympic bureaucracy had decided that the old gold, silver, and bronze medallions had "a feeling of mourning" with Nike, the Greek goddess of victory, sitting wingless beside a stadium, in a funeral pose. The new medal featured a full-winged victorious Nike standing inside a stadium.[6] That's more like it!

Many are surprised by the unpredictability of a lamenting person. "She is not herself." No, but how could she be? She is lamenting! Too many grievers have also discovered the predictable outcome of lamenting beyond the "window of remembrance" — friends may drop away. In the novel *The Secret Life of Bees,* the main character Lily lamented: "My mother died when I was four years old. It was a fact of life, but if I brought it up, people would suddenly get interested in their hangnails and cuticles, or else distant places in the sky, and no one seemed to hear me. Once in a while, though, some caring soul would say, 'Just put it out of your head, Lily.'"[7]

When advice gets weary. Most grievers have a moment when they tire of being bludgeoned by people giving advice, especially those trying to diffuse their lamenting. Ann Weems, whose son died on his twenty-first birthday, pleaded, "Come to my defense, O God. They're trying to tell me how to grieve. Tell them to leave me alone."[8]

There are many ways to chastise grievers. One writer wrote Miss Manners in a twit because a friend, whose husband had died a few months earlier, had kept her husband's voice on the answering machine. "It was very disconcerting to hear her husband's voice on the tape."[9] Miss Manners scolded the writer, "Oh, a new way to bother widows, just what we need." Miss Manners scolded those who want widows to stop using Mrs. and to get those rings off, rings the widow "has worn and cherished all her married life." Miss Manners would have none of it.

Advice can sound like scolding: "Your loved one wouldn't want you to carry on like this!" or "She would not want us to be sad." Father James Johnson, a friend of Truman's, counseled him, "I've learned the real reality of death comes only when your mother dies and then it seemed the bottom of our earth drops out. Yet we can't keep them forever. God knows best."[10] So if God knows best, does that mean God does not want us lamenting our loss? In 1853, Anne Garland, following the death of three of her eight children within several months, wrote Francis Burwell Carlett, "It seems almost too much for human hearts to bear without breaking ... yet I know it would be a sin to grieve too much for them."[11]

Lamenting requires attention to five needs:

- Lamenting the loss
- Making an account of the loss
- Voicing narratives
- Using rituals
- Extracting meaning from the loss

~ *Lamenting your loss.* In some cultures, wailing or keening is an allowable, sometimes expected, element in initial expressions of grief; in other cultures, a stiff upper lip is the norm. Remember the poise of the four princes (Philip, Charles, William, and Harry) and an earl (Spencer) standing stoically during the moment of silence at the beginning of Princess Diana's funeral. Stiff is not the word for their discomfort captured in pictures that communicated more than a thousand words. Millions watching the televised funeral, and a few inside the cathedral, wondered what an ex-husband and ex-father-in-law were doing center stage in the ritual? (Millions more had wondered when the queen was going to get around to acknowledging the death of the "people's princess." The queen's lament, under pressure from Prime Minister Tony Blair, was rather anemic.)

By contrast, a traditional African American funeral is emotionally expressive. The funeral unfolds without time constraints. Clergy work the mourners into a liturgical frenzy to better express their grief. That tradition, however, is changing as more African Americans become middle-class and adopt middle-class funeral norms.[12]

~ *Authentic lamenting makes folks uncomfortable.* Laments make folks uneasy. Few, even of those who profess deep devotion to the Bible, are comfortable with David's lament for his friend Jonathan. "I grieve for you, Jonathan my brother; you were very dear to me." Even a quick read leaves a low-grade uneasiness. Many wished David had stopped at, "Your love was wonderful," rather than adding the outrageous, "more wonderful than that of women."[13] Surely some warriors growled, "Say what?!"

David not only voiced his lament; he ordered that the lament be taught to and sung by his soldiers. Imagine the high-testosterone beefy machismo fellows sitting around campfires singing about the love of two men being "more wonderful than that of women." This warrior king's public lament was full-blown, publicly expressed grief.

Too many today are lament minimalists or are lament challenged. Others adopt Archie Bunker's admonition to Edith, "Stifle yourself!" Increasingly, women are expected to be "strong," at least in public venues.

When a lament gets loose it can be freeing. A priest friend of mine, conducting a funeral for a grandfather, asked if anyone wished to say anything. A grandson shouted: "I think it sucks!" Three people dove to cover the boy's mouth before he could offer more lament.

"No!" Father Gilbert countered. "Let this boy speak. This young man has said what is on a lot of our minds today. This death does 'suck.' It is unexplainable. Only this young boy had the courage to remind us." Turning to the boy, he said, "Young man, thank you for speaking so honestly. I bet your grandfather was very proud of you." This was not just a boy grieving a grandfather; the two had become pals since the boy's mother had become a single mom. Every day they spent hours together. Who would fill the gap in this boy's life now?

Laments are not always punctuated with tears or sobbing but sometimes a brutal honesty or a shared silence. Fred Gibson, my father's neighbor for forty-five years, and his wife, both in their eighties, came to pay their respects when my father died. My mother asked me to walk Mr. Gibson to his car. At the door he turned, trembling, tears streaming down his face. This usually reserved man declared, "Your father was like a brother to me. He was a good man! He was the best friend I ever had."

In Kansas City, Missouri's, inner-city neighborhoods, violence is epidemic. More than two dozen children will die this year, many at the hands of abusive parents or gang shootings. What if the next Colin Powell or Condoleezza Rice is living off Twenty-ninth Street? At one funeral of an adolescent killed in crossfire between gangs, a grief-stricken mother lamented not only with her voice but with her whole self as she screamed: "Stop this killing! Stop this killing! How many more mothers' hearts are going to have to be broken? Your mother, his mother? Young men, take a look at me. Do you want your mother to look like me? Then *stop the killing!!!*"

That mother's lament ricocheted off the walls of the church and undoubtedly remains with some of the adolescents who wore black that day.

~ **Master lamenters.** Sometimes extraordinary individuals can give us words that help. Mourners leaned forward to catch the comfort of Martin Luther King at the funerals for four young girls killed in September 1963 in the bombing of Birmingham's Sixteenth Avenue Baptist Church. "It is almost impossible," he acknowledged, "to say anything that can console you at this difficult hour and remove the deep clouds of disappointment that are floating in your mental skies." Then, leaning into the collective pain, above the sobbing, he confidently declared: "Death is not a period that ends the great sentence of life, but a comma that punctuates it to more lofty significance. Death is not a blind alley that leads the human race into a state of nothingness, but an open door which leads man into life eternal."

King understood hatred because, while his four children slept, the front portion of his home in Montgomery had been dynamited by the Klan. But for the grace of God he could have been sitting on the front row. Up to that point, his lament could have been said at almost any funeral. He turned his attention to the families: "And so today, you do not walk alone. You gave this world these wonderful children. They didn't live long lives, but they lived meaningful lives. Their lives were distressingly small in quantity, but glowing large in quality."

The sermon nearly over, the congregation lifted, King turned to the caskets, "Good night, sweet princesses. Good night, those who symbolize a new day. And may the flight of angels take thee to thy eternal rest."[14]

~ *Grief keepers give lament a voice!* Grief keepers do not nice-ify or pretty up lament so others will feel less uncomfortable. Grief keepers find ways to release words from the depth of their loss.

New York City fire personnel after September 11 voiced lament through traditional rituals with bagpipers, the outpouring of uniformed firefighters, and the presence of flag-draped caskets on fire trucks. Anguished laments were constructed and rehearsed in fire halls across the city. And sometimes, in late-night conversations, on rides back to fire halls, or around kitchen tables in the fire halls, informal laments were formed and exchanged. In the days following the attack, fire personnel stood in rituals and spoke laments to hushed audiences. Some read from notes; others spoke spontaneously from bruised, weary hearts.

I will never forget John William Perry's memorial service. Goose bumps snapped to attention at the bagpiper's first notes. The procession of police and fire personnel with the American flags brought tears to my eyes. A Kansas City congregation had gathered to lament the loss of a good man, a hero, a New York City cop who had been born in Kansas City.

When the first plane hit the World Trade Center, Perry was signing retirement papers in a police station nearby. After graduating from New York University Law School, he had become bored practicing immigration law and had joined the police department, serving as a beat patrolmen and as the chief prosecutor in the N.Y.P.D. Now, having put in his time, he was taking early retirement to start a law firm with his brother.

As the first reports came in to the station house, Perry tore up the retirement papers, asked for his gun and badge back, and headed out into the chaos. As John helped to evacuate the Trade Center lobby, he noticed an older woman having difficulty breathing and walking. John stepped up to her, signaled another officer to take her other arm, and promised to get her to safety. Then the building collapsed.[15]

The woman and the other officer survived. Officer Perry perished. As I listened to the eulogies and the music, questions darted about in my mind. How could this have happened to a man who had such a brilliant future?

~ *Lamenting publicly gives others permission to voice their laments.* Someone said that the ability to articulate ideas is what makes poets and sages. Someday, perhaps sooner than later, you will have to compose a lament. Your lament might be a model for other lamenters.

Laments may be verbal or written in an essay or poem. As John Corigliano did in the early days of the AIDS crisis, they can be expressed with the powerful music of Symphony No. 1. Or they can be sewn like the narrative fabrics of the AIDS Quilt. Grievers may lament through a letter to the editor in a newspaper, alumni magazine, or professional journal. Laments may be scribbled on a sympathy card.

Along with sharing stories, grief keepers keep a spirit present at a gathering with physical objects. Some families use photos, candles, or favorite flowers or artifacts and mementos — not to hide a vacant space but to enhance it. Some lament by letting the chair or space at the table remain vacant.

I heard a sixteen-year-old's lament during a Grief Gathering. His four-year-old brother had been killed when the brakes on the family van failed, and it rolled over the child playing in the driveway. While working with the young man, I could not get him to talk. At our last session, he brought a guitar and asked if he could sing a song he had written about his brother's death. I never recognized a melody in the angry strumming, but those stray tears that he paused to wipe away were an eloquent lament.

When he finished, the only words I could utter were, "Thank you." In that holy moment — and it was holy — a member of the group spoke.

"I liked that. I know what you're feeling."

"How could you know what I feel?" the adolescent snarled.

"I was your age when my four-year-old sister died. I think of her every day of my life."

The two sat staring at each other and then smiled; other participants sat, wisely, in silence. A lament had gotten loose in that place.

Whatever the format, give lament a chance to be voiced and received.

~ *Borrowing words of lament.* Vice President Walter Mondale stood in the Capitol rotunda to lament his mentor, former Vice President Hubert Humphrey. "Above all, Hubert was a man with a good heart." Across the years, thousands have downloaded Mondale's crisp words to jump-start their laments: "He taught us all how to hope and how to love, how to win and how to lose, he taught us how to live, and finally, he taught us how to die."[16]

One of the most eloquent laments I have witnessed was for Dorothy Culver. Allison Culver Keller, her granddaughter, then a high school senior, walked to the podium in the First Christian Church in West Lafayette, Indiana, and began reading words often attributed to Walt Whitman: "To laugh often and much; to win the respect of intelligent people and the affection of children." Then Allison, voice quivering, whispered, "I loved you, Grandma," and broke into tears. A wave of appreciative warmth broke over the congregation. How proud Dot would have been of her granddaughter in that moment. We could hear Dot's "Isn't she something!" It was not just the words; that quotation has been used in funerals far less effectively. Rather, it was a young woman's lament that her grandmother would not live to see her matriculate to her grandmother's beloved alma mater, Purdue University.

~ *Laments are not always expressed in words.* I can only imagine that moment, at the close of the funeral mass for two-day-old Patrick Bouvier Kennedy in 1963, when John Kennedy picked up his son's casket and cradled it tightly in his arms. The man who had stirred the world with a sentence in his Inaugural Address — "Ask not what your country can do for you, but what you can do for your country" — could not find words to express his grief. He may have been the most powerful man in the world, but the night before, at Massachusetts General Hospital, he had stood powerless and watched his son struggle for his last breaths. At the end all he could say was, "He really put up a fight, didn't he?"

The mass ended, the president seized his son's casket to his chest, a lament of action. Only a friend like Cardinal Cushing could say, "Come on, Jack. Let's go. God is good."[17]

Much has been written about John Kennedy's courage in facing down Nikita Khrushchev over the presence of Soviet missiles in Cuba. That hot August day in 1963, the president lamented a son unaware that in three months he himself would be the subject of a nation's laments.

~ *Making an account of your loss.* A small motel in La Jolla, California, has a picturesque lobby. I used to drop by to take in the expansive view of the Pacific Ocean and try my hand at the jigsaw puzzle that was always on a table. From time to time, a guest would walk by, study the puzzle a moment, pick up a piece, fit it in, grin, and walk away. There!

Grief is a lot like a jigsaw puzzle. Sometimes it is impossible to tell if a blue piece is sky, water, or a police officer's shirt. So the piece is tried in different connections. "My life feels like a jigsaw puzzle that I dropped while carrying its thousand pieces from the kitchen table to the living room. Now it's all over the floor and I know it must fit back together somehow, but it's an awful lot of work and I've lost the box, so I don't even have a picture of what it is I am supposed to be making. Mount Fuji or a charging elephant—which is it?"[18]

Grievers need permission to create, re-create, and reinterpret accounts of the events that led to the death of their loved one. Grievers need permission to audition their laments. Admittedly, some friends will listen once or twice and then become immune to the lament. In a restroom inside a stall, Sally overheard her grief critiqued by two friends.

"When is she ever going to get over it?" one demanded.

"I know. It's all she ever wants to talk about," the other friend added. "She needs to see a psychiatrist. My mother has lost a couple of husbands, and she still enjoys life, travels."

Sally thought about confronting the two ladies but chose to remain in place until they left.

"Account making is the way we spontaneously seek opportunities to tell and retell the stories of our loss and in so doing, recruit social validation for the changed stories of our lives," said Robert Neimeyer.[19] It is not about telling the story once or twice and moving on, but about retelling it until the griever is finished with it. I want to amend Lady Bird's wisdom from "People must be given the opportunity to hurt out loud" to "Grievers must be given opportunities to hurt out loud."

Lots of "ah-ha" moments come in mutual help grief groups when we recognize in another's lament a sliver of experience that fits ours. When the courage of another lamenter splashes and encourages us.

Some grievers wonder whether they did everything possible to save the life. What more could they, or anyone, have done? I have worked with caregivers who sacrificed around the clock, neglecting their own health, interests, marriages, and jobs to provide care. Some rejected offers of assistance. Some camped out by bedsides, fearful that a loved one would die in their absence.

Humor can be part of a lament. Although Barbara Roberts knew her husband was dying; she had to go to the bathroom. As governor of Oregon she was used to giving orders. "How could I leave his side now? What if he died while I was out of the room? I didn't know what to do. We had begun this long trip together and now only a few steps away from completion, I couldn't be gone at the moment he died. Tears welled up in my eyes. What could I do? Then I remembered what hospice had said about a dying person's ability to hear. So I simply told him, 'Frank, I have to go to the bathroom. You cannot die while I am out of the room. I want to be with you.' Frightened, I jumped off the bed, ran to the bathroom, and returned almost immediately to his bedside."[20]

In her brief absence, after four days without saying a word, Frank stirred and uttered Barbara's name twice. He waited for Barbara to return.

Due to physical, emotional, and spiritual fatigue, many grievers mimic Detective Lieutenant Colombo, looking for some detail that, had it been noticed at the time, might have altered the outcome. Many grievers cannot live with the unaccountable or unexplainable; some create outrageous explanations. Children, with poor lamenting skills, may blame themselves: "It was my fault that Daddy died." Rosie O'Donnell, ten years old, created a lament that her mother, weary of caring for five young children, ran away to California but "one day would return."[21]

Others lament the search for a cure or remission. A comforter listens, sometimes again and again as the progression of the illness is dissected, rehearsed, analyzed. Sequence does not change the outcome but it does restore order to remembered chaos. Some grievers have lived through roller-coaster progressions, right turns, left turns, and dead-ends in the medical treatment. Medical decisions may be reexamined. If only we had gone to Doctor X! Leading grief groups in a large medical center, I have pondered laments oozing with regret that a family did not come to the hospital earlier. "If only . . . " can be an essential starter for lamenting.

Some accounts are about navigating the bureaucratic bogs of modern medicine. The lament can be bitter when insurance was denied, delayed, or exhausted. Or if a hopeful procedure was deemed experimental by an insurance bean counter — and not covered — the lament narrative becomes darker; anger flashes. Often the griever must sort through a blur of medical personnel and procedures and, at times, colossal screwups.

 Who is listening? Grievers may feel that the key individuals in their lives become impatient with their lamenting. "They only want the high points," says Sarah, a recent widow.

However, much may be gained by another telling. The griever, in sorting through a fogged sequence of events, decisions, and mysteries, seeks to organize details into a coherent narrative. Sometimes a listener's question leads to an "Ah-ha!" A key piece of the puzzle finally fits.

Blessed are those who have listeners for their laments. Who listen again. And again. And again. Admittedly, some of the accounts, particularly of murder, suicide, or industrial accident, are ragged. Sometimes all the griever wants is agreement with their conclusion, "That was outrageous!"

Unfortunately, in this time-focused economy, time is money. Some lamenters hear the directive of *Dragnet* Detective Sergeant Joe Friday, "Just the facts, ma'am. Just the facts." Some grievers fear that too much bluntness will cause their listener to abandon or patronize them.

We owe grievers the gift of listening to their accounts. We must give them permission to tell their account verbally, as often as needed.

~ *People of faith have a responsibility to listen.* The German martyr Dietrich Bonhoeffer, no stranger to grief in World War II, wrote: "We must be ready to allow ourselves to be interrupted by God. God will be constantly crossing our paths and canceling our plans by sending us people with claims and petitions."[22] That is one way God arranges for Jesus's promise of comfort to be fulfilled.

Participants in Grief Gatherings often say, "I do not know how to tell you what I am thinking and feeling." If only I had a dollar for every participant who started a sentence, "This will probably sound weird. . . . "

To those who cannot herd their words into cohesive laments, I generally respond, "Have you ever played Scrabble?" Some are puzzled until I explain. "In Scrabble, you shake the cup containing the letters, dump out the letters, and then proceed to make words. So shake up your thoughts, and dump them out. We'll see if we can find some sentences and make paragraphs with them."

∽ *Voicing narratives.* Grievers need to tell the narratives, the stories, of the life they shared with the deceased, and its end. Some grievers do not want to focus on details of the dying or death. They want to concentrate on the life lived. "How did you meet?" They want to fit the death into a narrative in such a way that leads to the conclusion, "My loved one's life amounted to something." Or "My loved one made a difference." That was the genius of Dr. King's lament in Birmingham: the children's lives counted!

∽ *Using rituals.* Rituals have traditionally offered environments for lamenting. In our fast-paced culture, there has been an attempt to limit rituals roughly to a seventy-two-hour period. When people lived in the same neighborhood or community, death was a time to gather the tribe and friends quickly. Now family and friends may be scattered across the state, the country, or the world. "When is the service?" is an important question as calendars and Palm Pilots must be consulted and schedules juggled. Some ask themselves: "Did I know this person well enough to be inconvenienced by attending?"

Historically, three rituals were nonnegotiable: the visitation or viewing, the funeral, and the committal. Family and close friends were expected to attend all three rituals. In many communities, visitations lasted two or more days; friends attended each day. Due to the current pressured pace of life, many individuals consider ritual attendance a multiple-choice decision: I will attend one of the above — visitation, funeral, or committal.

Informal laments are exchanged when people visit. Increasingly, the committal is a family or private service. Who wants to be confronted by the final reality: a hole in the ground. So for busy consolers, the choice is between the viewing/visitation or the funeral; one, not both. No wonder the memorial service is growing in popularity — with the corpse in absentia — there is only one service to attend and it may be scheduled at a convenient time.

~ *Lamenting on special occasions.* Many grievers, particularly following a tragic or unexpected death, go through the initial rituals on emotional autopilot. Some are unable to remember who attended the service or various conversations. Some need additional opportunities to lament, particularly on anniversaries or special days when everyone else is celebrating.

Holiday gatherings present challenges to grievers because they tend to be very family oriented. Yet what is a grieving family to do with an absence that may be more keenly felt during holidays? Grief keepers have permission not to do holidays as usual.

Some grief-denying families opt for a full-scale holiday as a way to demonstrate that they have gotten over it. Others choose a modified, simplified event. Relatives and friends uncomfortable with grief may make pacts: "Whatever you do, do not say her name or bring up the time she..." Sadly, when some families gather, the deceased is never mentioned. No one says the person's name, shares memories, or honors a life well-lived. Too many go away saying, "There now, that wasn't so bad, was it?" or "We got through it without anyone breaking down. Good."

Grief keepers need to make room for the spirit of the deceased in the celebration by acknowledging the loss, symbolizing the loss, saying the person's name, telling the person's stories, and verbalizing a lament. Grief keepers recognize the holidays as a time to share a favorite memory or trait of the deceased.

~ *Partnering laments with others.* In Olathe, Kansas, on the Sunday before Christmas, parents who have lost children gather in a grove of trees near an elementary school and light candles to honor their children. Some people come alone because a spouse would not attend or found ways to be too busy. A few don't tell their family of their attendance. The gathering has no agenda other than to create a safe place for grieving parents to exchange laments and make space in the holiday frenzy for grief.

Initially, some participants feel strange. But as parents holding candles stand next to grievers who understand, emotional warmth spreads. For an hour on a December afternoon, they become a family of grief keepers. Over coffee and hot chocolate, they share stories and pictures, and Christmas becomes a bit more bearable.

~ *Hanging with traditions.* Sometimes we lament the loss of traditions as well as the loss of an individual. Some people create new traditions. One lady threw a twenty-fifth birthday party for her deceased son; family members and friends came, some with misgivings, and told stories and ate birthday cake. She asked me, "Was it all right to do that?" Not everyone has the strength to risk criticism.

Jackie Kennedy decided that John's third birthday party would go on. A few hours after burying the president and attending the reception with prime ministers, kings, presidents, and premiers, she and the Kennedy brothers and staff gathered in the family quarters in the White House to eat cake and ice cream and see John open presents. J. William Worden, a leading grief theorist, perceives adjusting to environments in which the deceased is absent a significant hurdle.

~ *Extracting meaning from your loss.* Some deaths are explainable: a heart attack, cancer, some physiological malady, or an invasive rare disease. Other deaths are mysterious. Why did the treatment not work this time? Why did he choose to drive this route rather than the regular way home?

The grief patrols seek to cut off any efforts at making sense of our loss. "It is not for us to ask why." Some have sung, "We'll understand it all, bye and bye," short-circuiting questioning. Maybe we will understand it later, but how are we supposed to survive now? What if the deceased was the person to whom you would have taken your uncertainties and fears?

Some laments become part of the stitching that holds our fragile lives together. Grievers lament their way into the answers they need.

~ *Lamenting through malpractice.* One reason for runaway malpractice suits is that they offer a place for grievers to lament — and a jury can be both moved and graciously generous. How does one find meaning in a death as a result of medical malpractice? Sometimes only in filing a lawsuit, which provides a thorough investigation into the factors that led to the death.

Not surprisingly, some September 11 families turned down the financial settlements and took their questions to courtrooms. In keeping the grief they wanted answers more than financial settlements. Kathleen Ashton, whose twenty-one-year-old Thomas died at the World Trade Center, believes that she will, someday, be reunited with him. "I need to be able to look at him and say, 'Tommy, I did the right thing.' The right thing is not to take the (government) money. The right thing is to try to get answers to see what sort of lapses allowed the murderers to do what they were able to."[23]

Some tragedies are on a national scale, covered obsessively, and periodically revisited, by the media. Others unfold quietly in communities and neighborhoods. I think of a father who retired from the mob to enjoy life, watch his grandchildren play, and putter in his garden. Until his son was killed in what the father believes was a payback from someone who had an unresolved dispute with him. A decade has gone by, and no one has been charged with the murder. Every year on the anniversary of his son's death, a memoriam notice appears in the newspaper. Of all the grievers I have worked with, I could not find a beachhead along the shoreline of this man's loss.

~ *Sharing your answers.* Sometimes we lament by trying to save others from having to lament a similar loss. Lots of babies died in the summer of 1963, but it was something else when the president's son died. Patrick Bouvier Kennedy's death became a turning point; suddenly researchers turned their attention to the effective treatment of saline membrane syndrome and other infant diseases. If the nation could send a man into space, surely scientists could help the weakest among us. Had John Kennedy been a sanitation worker in Boston or an accountant in Nashville, the loss would have been no less tragic, but it would not have attracted the attention of the scientific community. Today, only 10 percent of babies diagnosed with the disorder die. As I wrote this chapter, one of my friend's sons survived the malady. Thank you, Patrick.[24]

~ *Grief keepers make opportunities to lament.* Perhaps I have been too hard on Ferdinand Foch's thirty-minute episode of grief. Maybe thirty minutes was all he could manage at that time. Maybe there were other moments when he mourned his son, moments that escaped the notice of his staff and historians.

I have wondered whether Dwight Eisenhower, a student of military history, knew about Foch's example when David Eisenhower, his father, died during World War II. I found a stunning similarity between the two military leaders. Eisenhower did not attend his father's funeral. He wrote: "March 11, 1942. My father was buried today. I've shut off all business and visitors for thirty minutes — to have that much time, by myself, to think of him."[25]

On the long journey to a far place, give yourself permission to lament.

You Have Permission
to Be Angry at God

Where was God when my son died? Off listening to some concert by a celestial harpist? Skip that angel stuff! I want to know what God was doing at the time my son died!

— John, father of sixteen-year-old
who died in auto accident

The country held watch for eighty days as James Garfield lay dying of gunshot wounds he had received when Charles Guiteau shot him. The first physician to examine the president had assured him that the wound would not be fatal, but the president had challenged him, "I thank you, Doctor, but I am a dead man."[1] A second physician, Willard Bliss, was blunt: "Mr. President, your condition is extremely critical. I do not think you can live many more hours."

"God's will be done, Doctor. I'm ready to go if my time has come."[2] President Garfield's words were banner headlines in newspapers across the country. One composer adapted them into a song that would become popular, "God's Will Be Done."

Since it apparently was not God's will for Garfield to die immediately, the country faced a crisis, since the Constitution provided for succession only if the president died. Vice President Chester Arthur did not want to appear to be in any hurry to assume the presidency.

So the country waited until September 19, 1881, when Garfield died. His mother, Elizabeth Ballou Garfield, expressed the feelings of many when she groaned, "If he had to die, why didn't God take him without all the terrible suffering he endured?"[3]

That question, or some variation, is asked in thousands of hospital rooms, funeral parlors, and cemeteries every day. My mother repeatedly asked during my father's illness, "Why would God treat your father like this?" I pondered God's ways and timing as my mother died.

I have often said to grievers, "God can handle your anger." After my mother died a thought nagged at me: What if I have been wrong? In *Mature Grief,* Donna Schaper suggested, "For each of us, learning to relate well to God begins with recognizing the kind of God we have created in our heads based on our life experiences."[4] Sometimes, the god of previous comfort cannot survive a death. C. S. Lewis observed, "You never know how much you really believe anything until its truth or falsehood becomes a matter of life and death to you."[5]

Although C. S. Lewis experienced three griefs (the death of his mother when he was eight, the death of his friend Charles Williams during World War II, and the death of his wife, Joy), scholars and admirers have fixated on Lewis's grief for Joy. Joy's death, however, cannot be understood apart from the others. Each death sparked new understandings of God for Lewis. Following the death of Williams, Lewis reflected: "This experience of loss (the greatest I have yet known) was wholly unlike what I should have expected. We now verified for ourselves what so many bereaved people have reported; the ubiquitous presence of a dead man, as if he had ceased to meet us in particular places in order to meet us everywhere.... No event has so corroborated my faith in the next world as Williams did simply by dying. When the idea of death and the idea of Williams thus met in my mind, it was the idea of death that was changed."[6]

～ *Admitting grief.* I find freeing words in *The Book of Common Prayer:* "Almighty God, unto whom all hearts are open, all desires known, and from whom no se- crets are hidden, cleanse the thoughts of our hearts and minds, by the inspiration of the Holy Spirit, that we may perfectly love you and worthily magnify your holy name."[7] To some, cleansing implies an irritated parent scrubbing with a rough washcloth. I wonder if it might mean notice. God, notice my grief.

Many grievers fear that an honestly voiced expression of grief would grieve or annoy God. However, the prayer book text insists that God already knows about the grief and anger, so why not own it? Do we not offend the Holy Spirit, the Comforter, when we refuse to grieve because we do not open ourselves to receive the comfort the Spirit would offer?

Grievers can be angry and still perfectly love God. Grievers can be angry and still worthily magnify God's holy name. Jews have long understood that and re- cite kaddish following a death. The impediment to a relationship with God is denying grief.

The last verse of Genesis 2 has long fascinated me: "The man and his wife were both naked, and they felt no shame."[8] To stand in the presence of God, or anyone, and own our grief is an honesty that few experience. The Creator endowed humankind with the capacity to love and with the capacity to grieve, intentionally flip sides of the same coin. If we listen closely, grievers can hear God's question to Adam, "Where are you?" Unfortunately, many grievers keep reaching for fresh leaves to hide their nakedness, vulnerability, and powerlessness.

~ *Using anger as grief language.* Anger and irritability are languages grievers use to express the inexpressible. I counsel grievers, "God already knows, so you might as well go ahead and get the anger out in the open." God understands that you do not understand what you are experiencing. Grievers camouflage anger before they are ready to abandon it or before it has exhausted its creative potential.

In *Steel Magnolias,* Sally Fields, playing a grieving mother, fumes, "I want to hit something hard. Until they feel as bad as I do." Olivia Dukakis grabs Shirley McClain and offers her as a target, "Here, hit this! Knock her lights out, Melynn! Let her have it!" When Fields declines, Dukakis teases, "You just missed an opportunity of a lifetime. Half of Chickapin Parish has been wanting to take a whack at Weeza."

Have you missed an opportunity of a lifetime by camouflaging your grief?

~ *When God has to change.* Lewis Smedes faced a personal Golgotha when his son died "before he had lived the whole of a day." The death of his long-wanted child slammed Smedes into a collision with what he had long believed and taught and with the counsel he had offered grievers.

"Because of my Calvinism, God's face had had the unmovable serenity of an absolute sovereign absolutely in control of absolutely everything. Every good thing, every bad thing, every triumph, every tragedy, from the fall of every sparrow to the ascent of every rocket, everything was under God's silent, strange and secretive control."[9] That unshakeable certainty — in the face of other people's tragedies — had worked for Smedes until he tasted the salt of his own tears and watched his wife wracked with sorrow. "God's face has never looked the same to me since." In grief, Smedes faced a spiritual challenge: "I could not believe that God was in control of our child's dying."[10]

~ *Death challenges convenient beliefs.* When a tsunami slams ashore, it goes deep inland before receding. Nothing in its path is immune from its power. Grief leaves some of our most cherished assumptions as splintered as homes after a tsunami. "I could never again believe that God had arranged for our tiny child to die," Smedes later wrote, "before he had hardly begun to live, any more than I could believe that we would, one fine day when he would make it all plain, praise God that it had happened." Smedes added, "with one morning's wrenching intuition, I knew that my portrait of God would have to be repainted."[11]

Perhaps you have stood in the Sistine Chapel recently and marveled at the splendor of Michelangelo's mural, knowing what it looked like before restoration. Sometimes grievers must commit themselves to restoring their view of God; over time, another, more accurate image may appear. C. S. Lewis, in anguish following his wife's death, wrote: "Not that I am (I think) in much danger of ceasing to believe in God. The real danger is in coming to believe such dreadful things about Him. The conclusion I dread is not, 'So there's no God after all,' but 'So this is what God is really like. Deceive yourself no longer.'"[12]

110

Contrast Smedes's and Lewis's experiences with that of C. Everett Koop. Following the death of his son David in a mountain climbing experience Koop concluded, "God was able, but in His sovereignty He chose not to" prevent the death.[13] Not everyone can live peacefully with such a conclusion.

~ *"It is God's will."* The phrase "God's will" often gets bantered about following a death. These few words have the ability to bruise and batter some and, ironically, to comfort others. In 1862, Willie Lincoln died of typhoid fever, from polluted drinking water in the White House, following the biggest White House social event of the Civil War. Abraham and Mary hosted Washington's elite downstairs while two desperately ill sons upstairs fought to live. Willie died; Tad survived. In time, Mrs. Lincoln "came to see Willie's death as God's judgment upon her vanity, symbolized in the convergence of her party and his fatal illness." The nation had been scandalized by her spending, in wartime, on clothes and redecorating the White House. Mary Todd Lincoln concluded that Willie was "too precious for earth" and had been "lent" the Lincolns "to try and wean us from a world, whose chains were fastening around us and when the blow came, it found us so unprepared to meet it."[14]

You do not have to live in the White House to interpret a death as God's design to break the world's chains on a soul.

~ *A death can stir up questions.* Lizzy Keckly, Mrs. Lincoln's close friend and dressmaker, sat at the boys' bedsides during the ball. Weary from watching the boys suffer — and recalling the death of her own son early in the war — she was not present when "God called the beautiful spirit home." She did help bathe and prepare

Willie's body. Lizzy watched the president walk into the Green Room and lift the sheet off his son's face. She heard, "I know that he is much better off in heaven, but then we loved him so. It is hard, hard to have him die!" As Lincoln buried his face in his hands and sobbed, she wiped away her own tears.[15] An ex-slave and a president sat crying. It did not matter that he was president. He was a parent joining a hundred thousand parents like himself and Lizzy who wept for sons who had died and would die during the war.

God, in the unexpected places of our lives, notices grief. How do those who indict themselves for not having had enough faith to save their loved one's life experience God's presence? In the absence of a miracle, some spin an indictment: if only I had had more faith.

To continue to believe in God, in a good God, after a death, is a miracle in itself. Grievers must acknowledge the difficulty in believing now. Few are as blunt as Sheila Walsh: "If You took my son, I wouldn't doubt that You were alive; I just wouldn't talk with You anymore."[16]

~ *The world's best-known griever.* Job, one of the more widely known characters of the Old Testament, is generally associated with boils. Boils were only an irritant to him, however. The man lost ten children! Many fear invoking God's challenge to Job, "Who is this that darkens my counsel with words without knowledge? Brace yourself like a man; I will question you, and you will answer me."[17] The passage reminds me of my father demanding, "Well, young man, what have you got to say for yourself?!"

Job, described as "blameless and upright; he feared God and shunned evil,"[18] had seven sons, three daughters, seven thousand sheep, three thousand camels,

112

one thousand oxen, three thousand donkeys, and, fortunately, a large number of servants to attend to the requisite shoveling.

But Job's net worth unraveled in a gut-wrenching sequence of events. First, Sabeans seized his oxen and donkeys and killed those servants — except for the one who escaped to convey news of the disaster. While that messenger was still reporting, another arrived, panting, to report that "the fire of God fell from the sky and burned up" not only the sheep but the servants tending the sheep. While he was still speaking, another messenger arrived to report that the Chaldeans had raided and taken all Job's camels and killed all those servants.

After the audit of animal losses, the bottom dropped out. The Hebrew storyteller spins unfathomable chaos, "While he was still speaking, yet another messenger came."

"Your sons and daughters were feasting and drinking wine at the oldest brother's house, when suddenly a mighty wind swept in from the desert and struck the four corners of the house. It collapsed on them and they are dead, and I am the only one who has escaped to tell you." If they are dead, it was too late for Job to sacrifice for their excesses, as he had on other occasions. About this point many individuals would have grabbed their gut and moaned, "Oh, my God!"

"At this Job got up and tore his robe and shaved his head." He fell to the ground in worship, moaning, "Naked I came from my mother's womb, and naked I will depart."[19] In worship? How can you worship a God who has just dumped a lifetime of misfortune on you in the course of a morning? This was not some rogue wind, but the fire of God. God's fingerprints were all over these disasters.

~ *Grieving at this.* I will never forget walking into a home early one foggy February morning to encounter a moment of similar despair. I had been there often for a celebration of a birthday, graduation, Christmas, Easter, or for a hundred great meals. Nothing had prepared me to hear my friend, Dennis, the father, groaning, "Dear God, I can't believe this is happening! My boy is lying dead on the den floor!" while Buelah, the mother, a usually gentle woman, wailed. There was nothing I could do to deflect their pain.

I walked into the den and found Denny, an eighteen-year-old triathlete, sprawled dead on the floor. In the presence of an unexpected death, the biblical phrase, "at this" took on new meaning. (At this, Job got up and tore his robe and shaved his head.)

Throughout that day, I ordered myself not to fall apart during this experience; this family needed me. The questions I wanted to sling angrily at heaven would have to wait.

Dennis did not quote or paraphrase Job. He did not tear his clothes or shave his head. He did not lie on the ground in worship. He mourned.

Witnessing a father, mother, and brother mourning—not just that day, but as I drove them following a hearse to a cemetery, and later in the days and years ahead, they have allowed me to be a guest in their grief keeping.

Dennis says that a child's death is a parent's worse nightmare. From the Chaldeans and Sabeans you could, in time, exact revenge. But what are you to do with the fire of God?

To grieve, at times, is to revisit every idea of God that we have had. C. S. Lewis maintained that our flimsily secure ideas of God have to be "shattered from time to time." Sometimes "God does the shattering"[20] without, of course, obtaining our approval.

My young friend Elliott tends to make up game rules as he plays, generally to his advantage. Many individuals assume that we too can make up the rules. Others assume if one follows the rules or prays a particular prayer, God will bless them. Most prefer, as Donna Schaper contended, "a God who steps back and allows us to set up the world just the way we want it, and then says: 'Now that you've got things arranged just the way you like them, I'll do my best to keep them that way.' "[21]

In the faith tradition of my childhood, we affirmed, "If I live a holy life, shun the wrong and do the right, I know the Lord will make a way for me." If tragedy came, obviously someone had failed one or more of those three conditions. It's a spiritualized version of: Play by the rules, keep your nose clean, and you will get your generous portion of "and they all lived happily ever after." Moments of grief and personal despair challenge such thinking. Many grievers feel it happens disproportionately to kindly good people.

~ *What grievers have taught me.* Grievers have taught me about the boundary between whining and asking why. Grievers have taught me that questioning God sometimes needs more than a question mark to be punctuated accurately. ("Why" sometimes requires a series of exclamation marks as well.) For example, too timidly we read or hear Jesus's words during Lent, "My God, my God, why have you forsaken me?"[22] No; Jesus prayed, *"My God! My Godddddd! Whyyyyy have you forsaken me?!!!"* Jesus's exclamation marks shattered the bliss of heaven.

115

I have tried to capture Jesus's intensity but suspect it cannot be done without hanging naked, hands and legs nailed to a tree, abandoned by friends, bowels emptying down one's legs. My heart has never been sufficiently mangled to get the words right. But I have been around people whose losses have prepared them to offer a close rendition.

Jesus's cry of "why" echoes down through history. In the time it took you to read that sentence, "Why?" has been muttered, screamed, mumbled, and groaned in every language of the earth.

If it is permissible for Jesus to ask why — and for the Scriptures to include his query — then grievers have every right to ask, "Why?" Grievers have a right to confront God. To dare God to step into the ring of dialogue. "God, on this one, you have some explaining to do."

Those who have not experienced significant loss spout platitudes and certitudes about death being God's will. William Sloane Coffin Jr., after his son Alexander drowned, remarked that some who showed up to comfort early in his loss "knew their Bibles better than the human condition."[23] Coffin learned: "The one thing that should never be said when someone dies is, 'It is God's will.' Never do we know enough to say that. My own condition lies in knowing that it was not the will of God that Alex die; that when the waves closed over the sinking car, God's heart was the first of all our hearts to break."[24]

If more God's will-ers were challenged instead of tolerated as well-meaning, there would be more caution with the declaration. To be certain, some things are God's will. However, it is a marvel to me that more people dishing out "God's will" in funeral parlors and cemeteries are not pummeled severely. In a culture that Rowan Williams finds obsessed with "escaping or re-solving"[25] the unpleasant, this worn cliché infects the raw wound of grief.

Grievers have taught me to take my time before find-ing praise. I have heard some grievers comment very soon after a death or loss, "God be praised!" I have lis-tened to too many recitations of pious platitudes: "It is not for us to ask why" or "God never gives us more than we can bear." Someone did grievers a great dis-service when, having heard those words, they repeated them until they were grafted into the canon of Christian compassion.

In *Steel Magnolias,* when Darryl Hannah, a friend, starts in on Sally Fields, "We should all be rejoicing. Shelby is in the presence of her king," Fields interrupts the homily. "You just go on ahead. Excuse me if I don't join in. But I'd rather have her here with me."

Let anger rip. Let your laments loose, even if people around you have to dive for cover. If God gets to be Cre-ator of the Universe, occasionally he has to take stinger questions.

The narrator reports, "In all this [grief], Job did not sin by charging God with wrongdoing"[26] and "In all this, Job did not sin in what he said."[27] The narrator did not say, "In all this, Job did not sin in what he thought" but rather "in what he said." Perhaps, Job, like politicians, carefully selected his words.

Blessed are the grievers who have confidantes who can hear their unselected words and livid laments. Un-fortunately, these days too many grievers must rent a therapist's ears.

Grieving until death. Theodore Roosevelt experienced grief as a Harvard student, when his father died, and as a young New York assemblyman, when his wife and mother died. Seemingly, he had gotten those "troubles" behind him. He had, like many other grievers in that day, moved on with a new wife, more children, and new memories. He had charged up San Juan Hill as a Rough Rider. He had shot big game on African safari. He had reined in the monopolies. He had been a tough "Bully!" president. Biographer H. W. Brands observed: "When she [his first wife, Alice] died, he didn't simply put away his feelings for her; he walled off a wing of the emotional house in which he lived. He would marry again and become devoted to his second wife. He would overflow with paternal feelings for his children. But he would never again visit that part of his personality where he had courted Alice."[28]

There must have been nights in the African jungle, on the campaign trail, in the years after his defeat in 1912, or as he danced with his firstborn daughter at her wedding in the White House, when he thought about Alice. To his public, Teddy had gotten over her death. He had "taken it like a man." Then in 1918, during World War I, life ambushed him again when his son Quentin was shot down behind enemy lines in France. In that era of slow communications with the front lines, he agonized for days for news, any news until he received official notification from the army. Quentin, the son Roosevelt thought "a little soft,"[29] but whose shooting down a German plane had thrilled his father, was dead at twenty.

James Amos, Roosevelt's butler and bodyguard, recalled: "He did not weep or talk about it. But to me, who had been used to watch his every movement for years and knew him so well, it was plain that he was a changed man. He kept his peace, but he was eating his heart out."[30] At night Amos repeatedly overheard him groaning, "Poor Quenikins!" Roosevelt told his daughter-in-law Belle, "It is useless for me to pretend that it is not very bitter to see that good, gallant, tenderhearted boy, leave life at its crest."[31] Roosevelt, like Job, grieved the collapse of his dreams for this son. To another family member Roosevelt confessed, "There is no use of my writing about Quentin; for I should break down if I tried. His death is heartbreaking."[32]

Brands concluded, "Roosevelt never got over Quentin's death." In public, he could "put a stern face on his emotions," but "those closest to him could feel the anguish that made every action an effort."[33] On January 6, 1919, days after that first Christmas without Quentin, Roosevelt died. Although he had predicted that Edith would "carry the wound green to her grave,"[34] he did.

It will not intimidate God if you carry your wound green to the grave too.

How do you live with a God who does not answer your most anguished prayer? A God who, in Koop's perception, sometimes, chooses "not to" intervene?

~ *God's will.* No First Lady has tasted grief as extensively as Jane Pierce. (Franklin Pierce was president from 1853 to 1857.) Some might argue that Jane was not, in fact, the First Lady since all social responsibilities in the first years of the Pierce administration were handled by her aunt by marriage, Abby Means. The day after their wedding, Jane and Franklin left New Hampshire for Washington, D.C., so her husband could assume his seat in Congress — no honeymoon for this ambitious politician. Jane spent her days in a boarding house while Franklin spent days and nights learning the political ropes, i.e., drinking. During the next term she remained in New Hampshire, ostensibly because she was pregnant. In January 1836, Jane gave birth, but the child died days later. Pierce remained in Washington helping a constituent get a pension.

Historian Richard Shenkman commented, "Both of them felt the loss of their infant greatly, and felt the gulf that was widening between them greatly, too." The congressman found solace in a bottle. Soon constituents — and opponents — were whispering, "Frank Pierce is a drunk." Grief weakened Jane. She developed an illness, possibly tuberculosis, and wrestled with depression. Pierce, in Washington, "wanted his marriage to work, wanted Jane to be happy. But he wanted a success-ful political career more."[35] Besides, a wife could be replaced if she died.

Pierce's drive paid off. In 1837, at age thirty-two, he was elected to the United States Senate. Back home, Jane concentrated on sons Frank Robert, born in 1839, and Bennie, born in 1841. She began demanding that Pierce give up his Senate seat. In 1842, after he re-signed, the family had a blissful five months when he quit drinking. Then Frank Robert died in 1843. Soon thereafter, Jane discovered that though he had resigned a Senate seat, her husband now worked am-bitiously behind the scenes as head of the Democratic Party of New Hampshire. To keep his commitment to his wife Franklin Pierce did turn down another op-portunity to serve in the Senate and President James Polk's invitation to serve as attorney general. Without her knowledge he pursued the Democratic nomination for president in 1852. Jane fainted when she learned he had been nominated; in November when he was elected, a grief-stricken woman became Mrs. President (as First Ladies were known in that day).

Just after Christmas 1852, en route home to make final preparations to move to the White House, their train derailed outside Concord. In front of their eyes, thirteen-year-old Bennie was decapitated; neither parent was hurt. Shenkman noted, "There had never really been any chance that Jane would be happy as First Lady — but there had been a chance that she would at least be able to endure as she had endured her many other troubles. But after Bennie's death there was no chance of this at all. Merely retaining her sanity would be difficult."[36]

As deeply religious grievers, the Pierces grappled with questions about God's sovereignty. She, like Lewis Smedes a century later, pondered, "What's God up to?"[37] Few grievers can live with an absence of explanation for a loss. Initially, Mrs. Pierce concluded that God "had taken Benny away so that her husband could focus on his duties as president without distraction."[38]

That notion lasted until Jane had a long conversation with a cousin, Charles Atherton, the senator-elect from New Hampshire. Franklin had convinced Jane that the Democratic Party had drafted him, that he had not actively sought the nomination. (In those days women were shielded from the "unladylike" world of politics.) Atherton firmly rebutted that notion. For years, behind her back, Atherton informed her, Franklin Pierce had schemed for higher office. As she listened, Jane realized that her husband had not only broken his promise to her but had repeatedly lied. God took Bennie to punish her husband!

She had lost Franklin. She had lost Frank Robert. She had lost Bennie. Now she lost the ability to believe anything that Franklin said. Jane refused to attend the inauguration.

When she did move into the White House at the end of March 1853, she ordered that the state rooms be draped in black mourning crepe. Then Jane Pierce disappeared into a self-imposed isolation on the second floor, turning away all callers, sometimes including her husband. During the first two years in the White House, she appeared in public only once with Franklin. The White House became a tomb.

The grieving president became, in Shenkman's assessment, "a shriveled presence in Washington." The cabinet ran the nation. Soon whispers resurfaced that Pierce was drinking heavily. Although friends made allowances for him, as debate over slavery heated up, the Democrats needed a stronger candidate in 1856. Pierce was defeated for renomination.

~ *When anger is directed at God's field reps.* My friend Doug Manning insists, "Eternity will have to last a long time. I have enough questions to fill up a thousand years."[39] After I quoted Doug in one presentation, a woman challenged me: "Oh, no! If he gets there, his questions will not matter." Some individuals tolerate no questioning of God. In fact, grievers may unload their questions on unsuspecting clergy since, as God's field reps, they have no means for retaliation. Some ministers have volunteered for a challenge when they sought to rein in an honest expression of grief. Others have been recruited by a family member to "help" a griever move on or get over it.

I walked angrily out of a funeral for a mother who died young. She had just had her first book published, received tenure, and was teaching two classes she had created based on her dissertation research. She confided in one colleague, "I love my life! Everything has finally fallen into place for me." She had not counted on breast cancer. After musical selections, the minister, in a brief homily, acknowledged that he had once struggled with questions about the sovereignty of God, especially when he had to conduct funerals for the young.

"I used to ask 'why?' but God delivered me from that!" he declared. "I have chosen not to question why but to be thankful for the chance to have known this incredible woman." The inference was clear: if he, as pastor, had chosen not to ask why — neither should anyone else! He invalidated our grief! Hundreds of grievers, including a husband, her parents, three children, students, and colleagues, found their questioning of God doused because in that conservative congregation, "If Pastor says it, it is true!"

Later that afternoon I opened an angry e-mail. "Could you believe that crap? 'I have chosen not to question why!' If it had been his wife lying dead in that casket, if he had been left with three kids and one income, he would be questioning God. He would be mad as hell!"

~ *When anger is directed at God's people.* Some grievers are not angry at God but at God's people. Job endured the accusatory words of Eliphaz, Bildad, and Zophar far longer than I could have. The trio that initially had come to comfort him abused him when he would not cooperate with their assessment of his grief behaviors. I have listened to many grieving parents who recall words meant to comfort, that stung like salt along the raw spaces in their hearts and memories.

Too many of God's people miss opportunities to comfort because they cannot bypass opportunities to chide or set someone theologically straight. They volunteer to be Eliphaz the Temanite who clobbered Job: "Blessed is the man whom God corrects; so do not despise the discipline of the Almighty. For he wounds, but he also binds up; he injures, but his hands also heal."[40] Those razor-sharp words sound like a description of an abuser rather than a loving God. Eliphaz could not resist another jab. He predicted to a father who had just buried ten children, "Your children will be many; and your descendants like the grass of the earth."[41]

You do not lose a child and live happily ever after. I was moved by words by my friend David, penned following his son Dana's death: "We are surrounded by our memories and pictures of Dana and will cling ferociously to those while still living what is certain to be a different life now."

~ **The years after a death.** When concentrating on Job's boils, readers overlook the real source of his distress: his griefs. Many readers fast forward to the forty-second chapter of Job, "The Lord made him prosperous again and gave him twice as much as he had had before."[42] They seize this text to prove that Job moved on.

The narrator adds, "And he also had seven sons and three daughters." Also? Was this some make-it-up-to-you-for-all-you've-been-through consolation prize? While God doubled all the animals, God did not double the number of children. Nor did God replace the particular personalities of each child. How did Job answer the question, "How many children do you have?"

"The Lord blessed the latter part of Job's life more than the first" may be difficult for grievers to hear. Grievers want what they had. Grievers more likely identify with Flynn Kile, wife of Cardinal pitcher Darryl Kile, who said a year after her husband's fatal heart attack in 2002, "I'm not sure what will make it normal again. I'm still searching for something to make it right."[43]

Jane Stanford's son Leland Jr. died in 1884 and her husband, Leland Sr., in 1893, and she experienced six horrendous years battling the United States government over the estate settlement. She ignored the advisors who counseled her to close the university. In her latter years she invested her life in building not only a great university but in helping a small struggling church near the campus, Menlo Park Presbyterian. In relinquishing family control, she told university trustees, "Let us not be afraid to outgrow old thoughts and ways and dare to think on new lines as to the future work under our care."[44] That's sage advice for grievers to ponder.

It is what one does with one's grief rather than what one does about one's grief that shapes the latter years. According to a tired cliché: You get bitter or you get better. That is a choice grievers must make. Theodore Roosevelt ended his first wife's obituary, "For joy or for sorrow my life has now been lived out."[45] He believed that. God did not.

Grievers must, with God's help, make space for the memories of their deceased loved ones. Al Truesdale, writing about questions that surfaced in Oklahoma City and New York, contends that we "go back into the world and suffer in hope."[46]

~ *God makes no guarantees.* We spin dazzling but fragile sand castles in our minds, believing God will underwrite them. Instead God underwrites strength sufficient to meet life's demands. Donna Schaper has, as a minister, supported many through their anguished doubts and fears about God. She reflected, "God offers no guarantees that bad things will not happen, and no explanations as to why they do. What God the unfathomable and limitless One says is, 'I will be with you always.' "[47]

In grief, we discover that our notions, dogmas, beliefs, and expectations about God may have no foundation. But many grievers have discovered, to their surprise, that even when they did not stay close to God, God relentlessly chose to stay close to them.[48]

Lewis Smedes died while editing his memoirs. His daughter, Cathy, wrote a coda for the book, speculating on her father's first days in heaven as he and old friends and colleagues sat with God. "They ask questions and they receive answers. All the questions that Dad wrestled with — and that we all wrestle with — start to have answers."[49]

God offers grace to live . . . until answers come. Grief keepers have to be willing to live not in the absence of questions but in the absence of answers. God already had one Job. You do not have to be Job Jr.

On the long journey to a far place, you have permission to ask God, "Why?"

You Have Permission to Hope

The stories of those we love keep getting written, even after the loved one has died.
— Susan Ford Wiltshire, *Seasons of Grief and Grace*[1]

After Sir David Wilkie died at sea, his friend British landscape artist J. M. W. Turner headed to his studio and began painting his grief. Eventually when *Peace — Burial at Sea* was exhibited, art critics and patrons chided Turner about the darkness of his work, particularly the silhouetted black sails. Turner answered, "I only wish I had any colour to make them blacker."[2] Turner was not the last griever to be chastised for being unable to see and seize hope.

The early moments of grief can be the most difficult because the promises of a future filled with living happily thereafter, so valued in this culture, have vanished. In a grief-littered landscape, it is possible to find hope. Dr. Dillon Holt, previously president of Scarritt College, preached one of the most remarkable sermons I have ever heard, "Remember Lot's Wife." As Vietnam War protests were gaining momentum on college campuses, Holt's son, David, an Air Force pilot, had been shot down over Vietnam and the body had not been recovered. Holt was learning to live with the collapsed dreams he had long nurtured for his son. That Sunday, painfully aware that thousands of parents were hunting for hope as their sons died in an increasingly unpopular war, he read words from Genesis, "Then the Lord rained down burning sulfur on Sodom and Gomorrah."[3] Holt, a pacifist — which must have made for some interesting father-son conversations — compared the devastation in Vietnam to the devastation in Sodom and Gomorrah.

In acknowledging the complexities and surprises that can ambush a person — such as a son's death — this consummate preacher paused, then exclaimed, "Remember Lot's wife! She looked back on what she had lost and became a pillar of salt! You cannot live your life looking back on what you had, or loved, or owned. You have to look to the future. A future God will give you in his time. But if you become bitter, you will end up a pillar of salt."

~ **Looking back.** A temptation many grievers face is looking back. We long for the security or familiarity of relationships that once were and fear that the future can never be as good as what has been. Garrison Keillor captured the fear, "It's hard to make 'the best of it' when you know how good it's been."[4]

Millions of grievers have asked, "But how can I go on?" or "How can I live without...?" Even in the White House. In the early days of August 1914, as war broke out in Europe, Woodrow Wilson watched his wife, Ellen, die. He had once told Ellen that he could not live without her. Now he would find out if that were true. His daughter, Eleanor Wilson McAdoo, a newlywed, experienced those early days of the president's grief. "Woodrow's grief was so profound that he could not bear to speak of Ellen, even to his daughters. Only his sense of duty seemed to keep him alive. He worked all day and far into the night, grimly, often impatiently, as though nothing mattered very much. Margaret and Helen [his other daughters] saw him only at meals, sitting in deep, brooding silence, seemingly unaware of their presence."[5]

One evening, Eleanor went to visit her father. He could not be found. The staff thoroughly searched the White House. Finally, Eleanor walked into the pitch black East Room, groping for lights, and touched an arm — her father's. They paced the room in silence until he confessed, "I can't bear it. I can't think, I can't work without her."[6]

When Eleanor began crying, Wilson stopped her, "Don't cry. She was always so brave." Eleanor later noted, "It was as if he rebuked himself as well."[7]

Wilson could not see a future, even as president. He told a trusted aide, Colonel Edward House, that he felt like "a run down machine" and dreaded the next two and a half years until his term ended. In his emotional darkness he could not have imagined that within eighteen months he would marry Edith Galt. Arthur Walworth summarized the change: "The wistful widower who had dragged himself through the preceding winter by burying his mind in routine was now a bridegroom fit to fight wildcats. Political life had become again the adventure that it had been when he first took high office in New Jersey. His daily work seemed to him 'interesting and inspiring,' full of 'electrical thrills.' "[8]

~ *Fond memories.* Contemporaries Mary Todd Lincoln and Queen Victoria were famous for looking back. Mrs. Lincoln wore black for seventeen years after her husband's assassination. Queen Victoria ordered that the Blue Room at Windsor Castle be photographed extensively so it could be left precisely as it had been when her husband, Prince Albert, died on December 14, 1861. Hibbert described the daily routine: "She gave orders for Albert's dressing gown and fresh clothes to be laid each evening on his bed and for a jug of steaming hot water to be placed on his washstand. Between the two beds in the room a marble bust of him was placed; above it she had his portrait hung, wreathed with evergreens; and almost every day fresh flowers were strewn beneath it on the pillows. The glass from which he had taken his last dose of medicine was kept on the table... where it remained for more than forty years. On his writing table his blotting book lay open with his pen upon it as though it were waiting for him to pick up."[9]

The queen slept each night clasping one of the prince's nightshirts and a cast of his hand. When Princess Alice married, Victoria insisted that the wedding be held in the queen's private apartments, under the picture of Albert and the royal family.

During the first years following Albert's death, Victoria groaned, "I must try and live on for a while yet."[10] Victoria spent the next forty years making sure that no one in England forgot her husband, building Royal Albert Hall in Kensington and numerous monuments to his memory. As Lord Beaconsfield was dying in 1881, someone asked if he would be open to a visit from the queen. "No it is better not. She would only ask me to take a message to Albert."[11]

~ *Finding hope.* Grievers make spaces for their dead by remembering and honoring them. Tom Attig wrote, "By treasuring their legacies in all their many forms, we continue to love them. We cherish the memories and the stories of their lives. We care about what they cared about. We give them places in our hearts, souls, and spirits."[12]

A head-on collision in 1978, in which her best friend Sherry Morris was killed, forever changed Wilma Mankiller's life. Told that she might never walk again, Wilma fell back on Cherokee ways, choosing to think positively, "to take what is handed out and turn it into a better path." Initially she was not told that Sherry had died; once she learned, she wept so hard her own facial wounds hemorrhaged. Because her life had been spared, Mankiller felt a special responsibility to live life fully and authentically.[13] Long active in the Native American rights movement, in 1982 she was elected the first female deputy principal chief of the Cherokee Nation, and two years later Mankiller became the first female principal chief. She considered her grief and her recovery from her extensive physical injuries as a gift that prepared her for leadership.

~ *Finding hope in Hebrew Scripture.* One spectacular narrative of hope following grief is found in the Old Testament book of Ruth. In something of a paradox, the well-known words, "Whether thou goest I will go," once popular at weddings, refer not to the relationship between a husband and a wife, but between two widows: a mother and a daughter-in-law. Naomi, her husband, and two sons had fled to Moab to escape starvation during a famine in Bethlehem. The sons married Moabite women, and eventually her husband and both sons died. As a Jewish widow in Moab without a male protector, Naomi faced a stark future. She decided to leave, along with her two sons' widows.

As the trio journeyed, Naomi must have realized the two Moabite widows would have a stark marital future

131

in Israel since the Jews considered the Moabites cursed. Naomi vigorously urged each woman to return "to your mother's home" and blessed them: "May the Lord grant that each of you will find rest in the home of another husband."[14]

In a time without financial security for widows, to be left without children was devastating. Levirate marriage was the widespread practice; a young widow married her brother-in-law. Naomi knew, given her age, she would have no more sons for the women to marry. Orpah took Naomi's advice and headed back. Ruth, however, clung to Naomi.

Naturally, the widows' arrival in Bethlehem created a stir. Neighbors crowded in for a closer look. Angrily, Naomi blasted them: "Don't call me Naomi. Call me Mara, because the Almighty has made my life very bitter. I went away full, but the Lord has brought me back empty. Why call me Naomi? The Lord has afflicted me, the Almighty has brought misfortune upon me."[15]

Four times in her spiel, she blamed God for her griefs and the resulting economic chaos. No "God is good" in Naomi's worldview. In Hebrew *Naomi* means pleasant and *Mara* means bitter.

~ **Seeds of hope.** I wish we sent not only flowers to grievers but packets of seeds, as a symbol of a future. Grief keepers know that seeds come disguised in ways that encourage. Seeds may come disguised in a story. That is one reason many grievers read ravenously, looking for hope from someone who has survived or is surviving a loss. However, they quickly recognize writers who have leap-frogged over the pain.

Your experience as a griever, your words, in time, could make a difference to others who experience grief.

You might inspire others to hope. C. S. Lewis could never have imagined that his words on grief would be as valued as his *Chronicles of Narnia.*

Most of his adulthood, Lewis was a bachelor professor, scribbling words about fantasy kingdoms that attracted legions of readers. Through the response of one reader, that old stodgy Oxford professor discovered love. After reader and writer married, her cancer reappeared and challenged their bliss. After she died, in what he called his "mad midnight moments" — moments many grievers experience — he shaped his laments with a sharp pen. Many devotees may not know that his wife, Joy, was not the only loss in his life.

C. S. Lewis's life had been shaped on an anvil of grief. In August 1908, his mother died; his father was unable to comfort or care for his sons. Lewis and his brother soon found themselves "two frightened urchins huddled for warmth in a bleak world"[16] in a boarding school in Liverpool. Jack lost his mother and his home only to gain a headmaster's cruelty. One biographer commented, "Being completely under the power of such a brutal tyrant left Jack with an emotional scar for the rest of his life."[17]

In time, Jack found a seed of hope in writing and reading, and he retreated into a world of imagination. Those early losses would become the training ground for the genius of C. S. Lewis.

Just as he dealt with his mother's death through words, decades later he grieved his wife's death through his writing. Eventually those scribblings became his book *A Grief Observed,* published under the pseudonym N. W. Clerk because he feared readers — and peers at Oxford — would conclude that he had lost his mind. Legions of grievers have treasured *A Grief Observed*.

Attig contended that grievers "find and make meaning in ways that may not have occurred had we not suffered loss."[18]

In July 1954, Mrs. J. E. Theophilus wrote President Eisenhower, asking why her only son, David, had died on a routine patrol in "peacetime" Korea. "What has our country gained by his death and that of all these other boys?" No one, she wrote, was better qualified to answer her question. "You are a father, a general, and a politician, as well as our President." (She did not know that he was a grieving father.) Eisenhower responded, offering his deepest sympathies. He added, "Once having gone through the agonizing experience of losing our first born son, I assure you that my wife and I have some inkling of the suffering you now bear." Then he concluded, "Your letter inspires me to devote myself more assiduously to my own duties" as president.[19] How would he have answered that mother's letter had he not lost a son?

Grief keepers learn to survive and to thrive. Grief keepers find new ways to be or become themselves: "We transform ourselves as we reshape and redirect our individual, family, and community lives. Realizing that life cannot be what it was, we reach for new life even as we suffer. We establish something without precedent. We find new ways in day-to-day life. We discern possibilities and make new and fresh meanings in the next chapters of our individual, family, and community stories; we give them new direction and purpose. We build new connection to larger wholes."[20]

∼ Cooperating with hope. Writer Mary Higgins Clark, in her memoir, *Kitchen Privileges,* described the economic upheaval she experienced as a child when her father died. Her mother's response, common in that era, was to take in boarders. Mrs. Higgins made a new life for her family, but boarders altered the environment in which her children grieved.

Years later, when Mary became a young widow with five children, she found inspiration and hope in recalling her mother's example. In fact, Mary was juggling two losses. Her mother-in-law had often said that she didn't want to outlive her son, Mary's husband, Warren. While visiting when Warren was recovering from a heart attack, she collapsed at his bedside. Minutes afterward, Warren suffered a fatal heart attack. By the time the doctor arrived, in those days of house calls, both mother and son were dead. After the double funeral, Mary recalled, "I was beyond tears. For the moment, they had all been shed." Mary pondered her situation: "This is the rest of my life, I thought. I knew how much the children would miss Warr. My heart ached for them. I knew about all the birthdays and holidays and graduations when they would see other kids with their fathers. I knew because I'd been there."[21]

Although Mary had published short stories, she could not raise five children on that income. Five days after her husband's funeral, wearing widow's black, she signed on to write scripts for a radio show, *Portrait of a Patriot.* When an agent suggested that Mary attempt a novel, Mary began getting up at 5:00 a.m. and writing until seven, when she awakened the kids for school. How could two hours a day turn out a novel? Mary wanted a widowhood without regrets and if only's. "It was an itch I had to scratch."[22]

Three years later, her novel, *Aspire to the Heavens,* based on the lives of George and Martha Washington, was published. Over the next years came the good-selling books. Having financed the educations of five children, Mary decided she wanted to finish her degree.

One spring night in 1977, as Mary prepared to leave for her classes, her agent called. Simon and Schuster had offered five hundred thousand dollars for the rights for the hardback *A Stranger Is Watching* and Dell had offered one million dollars for the paperback edition. An incredulous Mary went to class and then drove home. "As I drove onto the Henry Hudson Parkway, the tailpipe and muffler came loose and began dragging on the ground. For the next twenty-one miles, I kur-plunk, kur-plunked, all the way home. People in other cars kept honking and beeping, obviously sure that I was either too stupid or too deaf to hear the racket."[23]

The next day, Mary Higgins Clark bought a new Cadillac. Readers today see only the literary and financial success and not the tough days as a grief-keeping widow with five children. Life was not given to her, as it is handed to some widows, on a silver platter (or even a paper plate). Daily she rehearsed her hope. She wrote, "a part of my being went dark and did not brighten again for thirty-two years, not until I met and married John Conhenney, my second spouse extraordinaire."[24]

Mary Higgins Clark demonstrates the wisdom of Frederica Mathewes-Green: "The only useful question in such a time is not 'Why?' but 'What's next?' What should I do next? What should be my response to this ugly event? How can I bring the best out of it? How can God bring Resurrection out of it?"[25]

I ask grievers to contemplate: "How can I cooperate with God to bring hope to this grief?" You may need to take down the No Trespassing signs and let others in on your grief.

~ *A narrative of hope.* That leads us back to Naomi, the angry widow. In Bethlehem, her daughter-in-law Ruth joined the barley harvesters. Her hard work ethic caught the attention of Boaz, the field's owner, who, realizing she was a widow, generously compensated her.

Then Naomi turned matchmaker. "My daughter, should I not try to find a home for you, where you will be well provided for?"[26] Urging Ruth to "wash and perfume yourself, and put on your best clothes," she steered Ruth toward the threshing floor where Boaz, the owner, was "eating and drinking and in good spirits." Once he had fallen asleep, Ruth boldly "uncovered his feet" and stayed the night.

The next morning, Boaz admonished a kinsman to buy Elimelech's property and thereby acquire Ruth as a wife (and Naomi). The man, weighing the complications, declined. Boaz acted immediately to take Ruth as his wife. The narrator noted, "The Lord enabled her to conceive." Ruth, at last, gave birth to a son.

Could Ruth or Naomi, early in their grief in Moab, have hoped for such a blessing? Could either woman have imagined the destiny of this child's descendants? The child grew up to be the father of Jesse, father of David, the great king of Israel. Naomi became the great-great-grandmother and Ruth the great-grandmother of a future king.

~ *Hope on the horizon.* Grief keepers wait for the first faint trace of hope in a situation in which others see only darkness. Sometimes a friend spots that hope in what appears to be chaos.

Greg Orr, as an adolescent, shot his brother Peter in a hunting accident, witnessed by his father and two other brothers. He described that autumn morning: "In the excitement after the deer fell, I must have clicked the safety off again and now, instead of pointing the rifle barrel at the ground, I casually directed it back over my right shoulder toward the woods and never even looked as I pulled the trigger. And Peter was there, a little behind me.... In that instant in which the sound of my gun firing made me startle and look around, Peter was already lying motionless on the ground at my feet. I never saw his face — only his small figure lying there, the hood up over his head, a dark stain of blood already seeping across the fabric toward the fringe of fur riffling the breeze. I never saw his face again."

The next moments would become the menacing memories of the future. "I screamed. We were all screaming. I don't know what the others were screaming, but I was screaming 'I didn't mean to, I didn't mean to!'" Greg ran across the fields toward the house where he blurted out to his mother that he had shot Peter, and then ran to the safety of his room. Later, his mother found him curled into a fetal position on the bed.

"Greg, it was an accident," she said softly, "It was a terrible accident. It wasn't your fault." How does a thirteen-year-old receive such words? "I started sobbing all over again. What she said made no sense. Of course it was my fault. Did she think I was stupid — that I didn't know what I had done, didn't know that I had done it? You could say that spilling soda was an accident, but you couldn't say that killing your brother was an accident. That was something far more horrible than an accident. Nothing in the word 'accident' offered me any hope."[27]

Orr admitted, "I had wanted her to hold me, but I couldn't say that. I had wanted her to forgive me, but I couldn't ask. I felt as if I had lost her love forever."[28] One week later, Greg went back to school, knowing that students were staring at him and whispering that he had killed his brother.

The Orrs went on. There was never another conversation about the accident. A few years later, his mother died as a result of complications of surgery, and Gregory was assailed by another wave of grief.

I had scanned a review of Orr's memoir without noticing the title, *The Blessing*. The blessing? How could any circumstance so tragic be perceived thirty-five years later as a blessing? Could Orr really believe that burden and blessing were two blossoms on the same branch? Yes. Grievers often discover a special gift of grace, in time, to see a blessing where others see only tragedy.

~ *"All things work together for good" as cliché.* Many grievers grimace when they hear Romans 8:28, the number-one spiritual cliché: "All things work together for good to them that know and love the Lord and are called according to his purpose." Although I memorized the Scripture as a child and kept it cued for immediate access as an adult, after witnessing its impact on fragile grievers, I deleted it from my comfort repertoire.

In some quarters, Romans 8:28 has a corollary. An individual says, "God is good" to which the hearer responds, "All the time." Then the hearer says, "All the time," and the original speaker responds, "God is good." Many people unleash these phrases without considering the impact on a grief-raw heart.

"God is good" can sting a griever like a slap on the face. What did John Kennedy hear when Cardinal Cushing told him to put down Patrick's casket: "Let it go. Put it down. God is good." "God is good" leaped off the page to one grieving father reading a draft of this chapter. He e-mailed me, "Yeah, that's what they tried to tell me when my son died!"

How can God be good in the death of twin boys? In the death of a thirty-one-year-old physician setting up practice? In the death of two couples celebrating shared birthdays when a drunk driver plowed into their car? In the death of two parents enjoying a summer afternoon dance? When cancer claims a young mother with two young boys?

God is good. I am just not ready to say "all the time."

I have come to trust my loose translation of Romans 8:28: "In all things, God will work exhaustively for the good of those who give him a chance to work."

Actually, Cory Aquino, a widow, taught me that principle. Benito, her husband, had been imprisoned over seven years in the Philippines on trumped-up charges of subversion and illegal possession of firearms. President Jimmy Carter persuaded Ferdinand Marcos that there would be enormous economic consequences if anything happened to Aquino. Reluctantly, Marcos released Benito to come to the United States for heart surgery. Benito had the surgery, and the Aquino family settled in Boston, where he taught at Harvard and M.I.T. The Aquinos could have enjoyed the good life in Boston, but Benito had to go back and fight Marcos's corrupt regime. On August 21, 1983, minutes after landing in Manila, Benito was gunned down as he disembarked. The grieving widow was on the next plane to Manila.

The hopes of many for a peaceful regime change had been dashed, although some opposition leaders toyed with a hope that Mrs. Aquino might unseat Marcos. For a day she prayed in a convent, obviously aware that the same people who ordered the killing of her husband could arrange her own killing. Who would care for their five children?

Hope exploded throughout Manila when she announced that she would run against Marcos. Initially, many commentators dismissed her decision as a symbolic protest. Marcos lewdly claimed that a woman's place was in the bedroom. Not to worry, he assured supporters, the only question would be the margin of victory. Still, the widow annoyed Marcos. He pulled out the stops to steal the election; thugs tried to intimidate voters and poll watchers.

On February 14, 1984, after the National Assembly declared that Marcos had been reelected, one million people protested in the streets. The cries of "Cory! Cory!" echoed through Manila. She asked them not to storm the Presidential Palace but to pray. Pray? In nothing short of a miracle, Marcos capitulated, and the U.S. Air Force flew him to posh exile in Hawaii.

Cory Aquino thoroughly believed in Romans 8:28. "God has a plan for all of us," she told a puzzled reporter from *Time,* "and it is for each of us to find out what the plan is. I can tell you that I never thought the plan was for me to be president."[29] Her Catholic faith convinced her that God could work for good in all things, including her husband's assassination.

So a botched third-world hit turned into a blessing for the Filipino people. Cory Aquino served four remarkable years as president.

God does not allow death to have the last word in a narrative of hope. Hope does not disappoint grievers who are willing to be surprised by the future.

~ *Finding hope in a son's death.* In 2003, I keynoted the International Conference on Care and Kindness and attended a banquet to honor recipients of the Crystal Cathedral's Crystal Wave Award. Up until the moment of the presentation, Adella and Fred Cooper were just two names in the printed program. That night I learned that following Adella's sister's death, the Coopers raised her four children. In 1949 the oldest, Robert, learning to drive, made a misjudgment and drove into a tree and was killed. The Coopers believed that there had to be a way young drivers could learn to judge road conditions. Using insurance money and cars donated from the local Ford and Chevrolet dealerships, the Coopers, in their grief, created the first driver education program in the state of California, an idea that caught on and became a nationwide program. Out of Robert's death came a blessing that continues to bless others by preparing adolescents to drive. The Coopers told me in an interview, "We did what we did where we were with God's help. He helped us go on." God helped the Coopers take the sting out of Robert's death.

The question is not "How can it be a blessing?" but rather "How can it become a blessing?" Greg Orr answered critics: "How do I dare to say my brother's death was a blessing? Can I keep my own nerve long enough to work my way through the strangeness of that word?"[30]

~ *Responding with hope.* At the Jonesborough story-telling festival, storyteller Don Davis told about a woman who faced multiple challenges. After her oldest son developed AIDS and she had chosen to care for him, her husband left. She lost so many days of work that she lost her job. After she lost her job, she lost her house. Then her son died. Her pastor asked her, "With all that has happened to you, how do you get out of bed every day?"

"Oh, pastor," she replied, "I vote every morning."

"You vote?" the pastor sputtered, dumbfounded by her answer.

"Yes, I vote. As soon as I wake up I say, 'All in favor of having a good day say Aye. Those opposed say Nay. The ayes have it. The motion carries. This is going to be a good day!' Then I get out of bed and have a good day."

Mark Moore, who experienced death and grief as a prisoner of war during World War II, once told me, "It's not so much what happens to you, as how you choose to respond." Initially, that sentence sounded outrageously simplistic. Yet over the years that thought became a guiding philosophy of my life. It is not so much what happens but how one chooses to respond. How you honor your grief will shape the outcome. Multitudes of women lost husbands during the Civil War; few imitated the mourning behaviors of Mary Todd Lincoln. Lots of fathers lost sons in 1921; few kept the grief as did Dwight Eisenhower.

In 1999, Gladys Staines, a missionary in India, learned that her husband, Graham, and her sons, Philip, ten, and Timothy, eight, had burned to death after Hindu rebels had set fire to the jeep in which they were sleeping. In the Indian state of Gujarat, several thousand people died in the conflict between Hindus and Muslims. Gladys Staines could have moaned, "I am out of here," and returned to rebuild her life in Australia. Instead, she chose to stay in India and run a leper colony. Early in her grief, if you had suggested that someday she would be recognized as one of India's leading peacemakers and would win the prestigious Gandhi Communal Harmony Award, Gladys Staines would have shaken her head in disbelief. Yet in 2002 her work in building harmony was recognized.[31] Gladys chose to identify "with women like me who have lost their children, maybe in accidents. Natural calamities." And she admits that memories of her husband and sons are "never too far away."[32]

A deeply depressed twenty-six-year-old male considered suicide after the death of the love of his life, Ann Rutledge. If you had whispered, "You can't do this. Someday you will emancipate the slaves," would Abraham Lincoln have believed you?

A fifty-year-old man's mother died. Two months later his two-year-old daughter died. Weeks afterward his brother-in-law committed suicide. If you had said, "You will lead England during the darkest hours of a world war," could Sir Winston Churchill have believed you?[33]

Grief keepers believe there will be a tomorrow, without being certain when tomorrow will arrive.

Anyone can be bitter like Naomi. But what will you do with that anger? After her daughter's murder, Charlotte Zillinger decided: "If life experiences are not used, they are wasted."[34]

∼ *The story is not over.* Grief keepers acknowledge the suspension of ordinary time. Hours now have more than sixty minutes, days have more than twenty-four hours. Death has a way of reprioritizing one's plans, desires,

144

wishes, mission statements, fantasies, and Day-Timers. Some find it simpler to pull the covers over their head or to repeat the words Eleanor Roosevelt used to dismiss reporters' questions about her future, "The story is over."

For forty-seven years, Mamie Till Mobley tended her hope that justice would be done in the death of her son. Emmett, thirteen, had gone south from Chicago to spend some of the summer of 1955 with relatives in Mississippi. Responding to a peer's dare, he flirted with a white woman, allegedly calling her "baby" and whistling at her. Her husband and brother-in-law came for Emmett in the middle of the night. His body was eventually fished out of the Tallahatchie River. What started out as an ill-advised adolescent prank ended up with torture, mutilation, and murder. An eye was gouged out, an ear was missing, and he had a bullet hole in his head.

Although everyone urged her to close the casket, Mamie rejected that advice. Four days later at a Chicago funeral home, thousands passed Emmett's casket. Mamie explained her decision: "I wanted the world to see what I had seen. I wanted the world to see what had happened in Mississippi. I wanted the world to see what had happened in America." *Jet* magazine ran a picture of Emmett's bloated face. Leonard Pitts Jr. remembered his initial response to the picture. When you saw that picture you knew why "coffins have lids."[35]

It wasn't just the murder that troubled Mamie but the fact that a jury of twelve white men had seen the pictures, heard the witnesses, and after less than an hour of deliberation had returned a not guilty verdict! Mamie died hoping that justice would someday be done. Many said that she wasted those years, that she could have moved on and had a different life.

Leonard Pitts disagreed. "She spent forty-seven years speaking, writing and agitating in the name of her murdered son."[36] That *Jet* picture, periodically republished, and a mother's unresigned hope encouraged a lot of individuals to work for justice in their tragedies.

Mamie could have buried, camouflaged, or deep-sixed her grief. Lots of parents have. Rather she chose to keep her grief, even when it annoyed, irritated, and angered others, including family members.

Emmett Till has not been forgotten, thanks to the determined grief of a soul-wounded, grief-keeping mother. When Mamie died, newspapers across the country reopened the story, and another generation learned about Emmett Till.

Sometimes grieving takes more than just prophesying hope. Helpers have to get involved, sometimes in messy work, to help the seed of hope take root in a griever's heart. By saying no to the world's agenda to move on and get over it, grief keepers say yes to hope.

On the long journey to a far place, give yourself permission to hope.

You Have Permission
to Name Your Loss

Some went away. I irritated them. I wanted to talk about Mark. They got tired of listening. Get on with your life, they said. No, they did not say it, but they meant it.

— Susan Sonnenday Vogel, *And Then Mark Died*[1]

It may have been cold that January 1880 night, but it did not deter the man walking up and down Twenty-ninth Street, talking and crying with his cousin Tom Murphy. That afternoon he had buried his forty-two-year-old wife. The political establishment — the governor, members of the legislature, and countless politicians — had turned out. His soul, however, was burdened. He knew that he had allowed politics, especially the last seven years, to overshadow his marriage; Ellen had suffered with his late hours and constant travel.

The remorse would never fade for Chester Arthur. If anyone had predicted that within twenty months he would be president of the United States, it would have been just as unbelievable as the idea, twenty months earlier, that he would be a widower.

In those days a man, particularly a politician, was expected to put a wife's death behind him. And to move on. To remarry. Eight months after Ellen Arthur's died, General Arthur was named Garfield's running mate on the Republican ticket. When he returned home from the convention, while at a family gathering, his eight-year-old daughter, Nell, asked an aunt what she could do to congratulate her father. Her aunt suggested giving him some flowers. As the jubilant Arthur kissed her he broke down, saying, "There is nothing worth having now." His biographer, Thomas Reeves, captured the moment: "Arthur's continuing grief over the loss of his wife, intensified by an honor she would have cherished, remained a secret to all but his family and intimate friends."[2]

The day Garfield died, Vice President Arthur spent the day at home in New York City. At 11:30 p.m. he was notified by telegram of the president's death. Immediately, reporters knocked on his door asking for a statement. His doorkeeper, Alex Powell, was clear: "I daren't ask him. He is sitting alone in his room sobbing like a child, with his head on his desk and his face in his hands. I dare not disturb him."[3]

How different everything would have been, Arthur told friends repeatedly, if his wife had been there to support him. "Honors to me now," he confided in Brodie Herndon, "are not what they once were."[4]

Perhaps you have spent time turning the pages of picture books with a child as you tested the child's recognition skills. Pointing to particular animals, you asked their names. I love to misname animals and draw out the child's protest, "No! That's a rabbit!" and their "You should know better" look. Children must learn the names of people, animals, and objects in order to express their needs and wants. Grievers must learn to find the words to express their grief, to name their loss.

~ *Learning to name life's experiences.* Genesis reports that God paraded animals by Adam to see "what he would name them." This was not a casual chat time between the Creator and the creation. "Whatever the man called each living creature, that was its name."[5] What Adam did with animals, grievers must do with their loss.

Naming our loss is an empowering way of managing grief. Naming a loss has a critical role in dealing with life's crises, experiences, and griefs. Gary Egeberg observed, "When my life becomes too complex, naming helps me regain simplicity and clarity."[6]

Grievers commonly find themselves speechless, unable to corral words to express their loss. I recommend that grievers audition words to name their experience. Sometimes powerful words are needed. When I asked Gladys, age seventy-eight, who was grieving over the death of her husband, how she felt, she snapped, "Like shit. Oh, no," she gasped. "Oh, no, I meant to say . . ."

"Gladys, I have been around enough grievers to understand the word. Sometimes it is the only word that works."

Many grievers have to carefully select their words and edit their experience to fit in with some grief groups or to keep the support of caring friends. At St. Luke's Hospital, many grievers let their words fly with abandon.

In mutual help groups, I often witness the naming process. Strangers walk into a room, usually nervously. Over the next six weeks, they work on naming their own grief, and they also support the naming experiences of others. Frequently they recognize something they have been trying to express in another's words. "Could you say that again, please?" Another person's courage to speak honestly gives some people the strength to release their own words, perhaps for the first time.

Grievers who keep silent miss the opportunity to express the extent of their grief.

In one group, Cheryl struggled as she listened to people who had lost mothers, husbands, stepfathers, and children. In the first session, following my request, she did the initial disclosure asked of all participants: her name, the name of her loved one, when the loved one died, how the loved one died, and what brought her to the Grief Gathering. Cheryl was grieving the loss of her partner of five years who had died after a long illness. Some people in that circle had never known a lesbian. Although Cheryl contributed modestly to the discussion, she was afraid any further revelations would be rejected.

One particular evening, I was frustrated as facilitator. The group did not seem to be responding. I offered a final question, "What are you going to do on Valentine's Day?" which was four days away.

"I am going to the cemetery," one participant replied. Others acknowledged plans or tentative plans.

Then Cheryl snapped, "What if you don't have any place to go? I do not have any place to go on Valentine's!" Her vehemence resounded like a clap of thunder.

"What do you mean you have no place to go?"

"She was cremated, and her family has the ashes!" The family had stepped in at the partner's death and taken charge. They made it clear that Cheryl had no say now. Cheryl's story rushed like a swollen stream into the circle. The family had not allowed her to attend the funeral. The funeral director even slammed the door in her face. Her sympathy card was returned. The group was stunned.

"You don't understand," Cheryl sobbed. "This is Kansas City. Lesbians have no rights!"

"So, Cheryl," I asked, "what are you going to do? How are you going to keep your grief on Valentine's Day?" When she replied that she didn't know, I asked, "Are you open to suggestions?" She was.

"You were together five years. How about buying five balloons, red or pink for the day, going to the important places in your relationship, and either leaving a balloon or releasing a balloon in that important space." Cheryl pondered the suggestion. Like so many, she had needed a safe place to name her grief.

∼ *An avalanche of clichés.* In this culture, members of the grief patrol keep their move-on admonitions cued up. "Nothing you can do . . . get over it . . . don't cry over spilled milk." Some grievers have become so used to being dished a large portion of cliché that they will not risk naming their loss. Earl Cavanaugh, dean emeritus of Grace and Holy Trinity Cathedral in Kansas City, once said that we live in "the age of soft clichés." Unfortunately, the recipients of our cliches "have a different coinage for those same words."[7] Clichés are hurtful, though they do not leave visible welts.

This grief-dodging culture is addicted to clichés. Any day I expect to see a McDonald's-like sign proclaiming, "Clichés. Billions dished out daily." Clichés dowse the naming process. Few challenge the dispenser. Some grievers actually mutter, "I will try to do better."

Repeatedly grievers say, "If I hear one more person tell me to get over it, I am going to scream!" I respond, "Go ahead and scream!"

∼ *Naming the real relationship.* Sometimes the underbelly of a relationship has to be acknowledged.

Not every deceased person is a loved one. Not every marriage is a good marriage. Not every parent-child relationship is tender. Grievers need safe spaces to acknowledge the real relationships, estrangements, dysfunctions, and longings they had with the deceased.

Some grievers need to admit that they spent their whole lives trying to get a molecule of love or affirmation from a parent. Some finally need to let go of a cherished fantasy of a last-minute whisper, "I love you, too."

John, on his first night in a group as a widower, told participants he had had a great marriage. By week three, it was a good marriage. Finally, believing he could trust the other grievers, he confessed, "It wasn't a good marriage. I am supposed to be grieving, but I'm not. Unless I am grieving for what never was." For many grievers a huge gap exists between PMI and PMR, between the public marital image and the private marital reality.

Warren Harding, president of the United States, died in San Francisco, on August 2, 1923, under mysterious conditions. There was no autopsy. By October, Washington, D.C., was rife with rumors about corruption in the Harding administration, and the Teapot Dome scandal began leaking to the press. Rumors persisted that the president had been poisoned. To squelch the rumors, Mac Jennings, a family friend, with the permission of the former First Lady, took on the rumors. "I want . . . to give lie to the absurd and vicious story that he was the victim of a poison plot. There is not a shadow of foundation for this canard."[8] However, no further details of the president's death were disclosed. Mrs. Harding, as his widow, had a crisis on her hands: her husband's reputation was deteriorating.

Florence Harding wrote Harry Daugherty, a family friend, "[I am] rearranging my life as I inevitably must." Her biographer, Carl Sferrazza Anthony added, "Florence determined that having 'laid the dead to rest,' she must 'devote herself to the living' and ignored social expectations that she indulge in mourning."[9] She knew that she would be compared to the two other living widows of presidents, Nellie Taft and Edith Roosevelt, and, six months later, Edith Wilson. Ray Clipper commented, "Mrs. Harding, always a most practical, capable woman, for all her feminine charms, approaches her new life just as she has the past difficult tasks or trying situations, with a determination to make herself mistress of the situation rather than let it make her."[10]

Many grievers want to be mistress (or master) of their grief. Few like the sense of powerlessness that grief brings. One unidentified Senate wife observed of Mrs. Harding, "I think of her most pitifully as she came back to Washington to get Warren's papers from the White House, read them over word by word, discovering at last the things she had only guessed." Frank Doubleday, head of Doubleday Publishing, approached her about a potential biography of her husband. Florence Harding told him that she had burned the president's papers because she "feared some of it would be misconstrued and would harm his memory."[11] She did not disclose that she was still reading and burning documents.

~ *Maintaining the fiction.* In some cases, it is not the grief that taxes the griever's strength and energy; it is the fictionalizing. Jennifer Elison and Chris McGonigle, in *Liberating Losses,* describe a client who said on his first visit, "You're going to make me forget about my wife, aren't you?" Hardly. Although many grievers have forgetting on their agenda, Elison and McGonigle contend, "The task of grieving well is not about forgetting but about remembering in life-giving ways."[12]

Elison and McGonigle continue: "Surprisingly, indifference to a death can point to unfinished business, too . . . it may mean feelings are being repressed. Even if the marriage was cold, or the relationship unloving, we need to grieve what we didn't have and what will never be possible now. The grief is, many times, much greater for what we wish we'd had."[13]

In order to name their loss, some people must write a personal eulogy; some must compose a dissenting eulogy. Rabbi Marc Gafni pointed out, "There is no statute of limitations on a eulogy. The eulogy should not be a glossy finish or a whitewash for a complex and colorful life. . . . A eulogy should be words to portray as accurately and lovingly as possible the measure of a person's depths."[14] The key, of course, is to be as accurate as possible.

I have wondered what it was like for Florence Harding, six months after her husband's death, to sit behind the Calvin Coolidges and the latest First Widow, Edith Wilson, at the service for President Woodrow Wilson in the National Cathedral — a grand liturgical experience. Florence had told the minister who presided over Warren's service, "Keep it under thirty minutes." Sometimes another's funeral ritual offers a chance to revisit and perhaps to rename our own finished relationship.

~ *When naming is difficult.* Naming a loss brings it into focus. That's why grievers talk to counselors or linger over coffee with someone else who has experienced a similar loss. They hope to find additional ways to name their loss, to fit another piece into the puzzle of grief.

Honestly naming a loss makes some individuals, even close friends and family members, uncomfortable. Some individuals will not name their grief in their own family. Group participants will tell virtual strangers things they have never told a spouse, a parent, or a sibling.

"If I abruptly hang up," a grieving mother whispered to a grief hotline counselor, "it means my husband has come home. He does not want me to talk about it. Ever." Family members have been known to scold, change the subject, or leave the room when the subject of a particular death comes up.

Spouses who come to the first meeting of a support group sometimes do not return because talking about their grief is too tough, too demanding, or, ironically, too freeing. If only they could experience Gary Egebert's conclusion: "Naming reduces the power the unnamed has over us."[15] Families that can name their dead — saying the name and telling their stories — are healthier than those that don't.

~ *Naming the secrets.* Too many grievers think they should speak no ill of the dead, should not relinquish custody of any secrets. Carolyn Koons dared to name a secret. Her father, Cliff, had been outrageously abusive to her. Repeatedly, he had threatened to kill Carolyn when she was a child; her mother had been the barrier between them. With her mother's death, Cliff's threats

155

became more menacing. Then, one day in 1977, when Carolyn was now a college professor, the university operator relayed a message to her: "Tell Carolyn that her dad called and that I'm on my way, and this time it's for good." Cliff had never acknowledged his daughter's achievements in the field of Christian education during her career at Azusa Pacific University nor those of his grandson, Tony, whom she had adopted. As Carolyn grabbed her car keys to flee from campus, she asked herself: "Why was I still running from my father's anger, and why was he still haunting me? It seemed so senseless. His hatred for me had already ruined his life. Why was he so intent on ending mine? I had walked out of his life years ago. I'd let go. Why wouldn't he? Why wouldn't he just leave me alone? He'd terrorized all but the last fifteen years of my life. This time he was finally going to kill me."[16]

Clifford Arthur Koons had a stroke while driving to the campus. Eventually her brother called with the news that Koons had died of alcohol poisoning. "There was silence over the phone lines as the pronouncement sank in. I didn't feel anything at all. He'd been there — violent and mean — every single day of my life. How could he and his threat just disappear, vanish like that?"[17]

Only seven people attended Cliff's funeral in a chapel at the mortuary. The minister chose to name the family's secret: "I am sure that many of you today come to this memorial service for Clifford Arthur Koons with mixed emotions. Some of you may feel tremendous anger and bitterness, others sheer relief in knowing that Cliff Koons, who so dominated your life over these years, is no longer among us. To perhaps one or two of you, today may bring confusion and an onrush of painful memories. Just maybe in some of you there might be just a little sorrow for this tragic man and his life."

There was no faux sentimentality that afternoon. The minister continued his brief homily with a challenge: "Cliff Koons was a lonely man and an angry one, who made some choices in his life that trapped him — leaving him with years of repeated sins and pain. He basically came to the end of his life empty-handed, but you, ah, the seven of you still have your lives ahead of you. You still have choices to make."[18]

Carolyn chose to name her relationship with her father in conference presentations. I had worked with her in several settings and knew she had a remarkable story that could help others find the freedom to name their challenged family relationships. I nudged an editor friend to hear her. He did and asked her to write her story. In her book she told her story without whitewashing it.

Carolyn's story has freed many other people to be able to name their griefs. Naming your own grief could be equally empowering.

~ *Naming the God who seems absent.* For some grievers, God's involvement or his absence in the dying or death of their loved one or his silent absence during their grief has to be named. "God may have promised good," one friend said after her son's death, "but I sure don't see any evidence of it." I saw the comedy team Hicks and Cohagan perform a sketch about a man who wants to file a lawsuit. Stephen Hicks, playing the lawyer, asked his prospective client, "Okay, who do you want to sue?"

"God," Jerry Cohagan answered straight-faced.

"Did you say, God!? On what charge?" Steve sputtered.

"Breach of contract. He hasn't been God."

The audience laughed outwardly, but some understood the sketch on an inner level. Many grievers feel God has been absent or negligent.

The son of a friend of mine has a very imaginative prayer life. The child, alarmed by the threat to children in Iraq during the war, prayed one night, "God, you need to do a better job of Goding." Many grievers have thought that, though few have dared to verbalize it. Not everyone has the courage to scream, "God, where were you?" Ann Weems demanded:

> Undo it, O God!
> Give him back![19]

In my own time of grief, I composed a griever's verse to "Amazing Grace":

> In grief's long hours I shall not fear
> God will companion me.
> He'll hear my troubled prayers and pleas
> And still my grieving heart.

God accompanies us in life's unbelievable and unexpected moments. Matthew Bridges said it in the nineteenth century in his anthem "Crown Him with Many Crowns":

Crown him the Son of God, before the worlds
began,
And ye who tread where he hath trod, crown him
the Son of Man;

158

Who every grief hath known that wrings the human
    breast,
And takes and bears them for his own, that all in
    him may rest.

Grief cannot be integrated in the absence of truth.
The only truth that will do is the honest-to-God variety,
which may leave friends and family diving for shelter
and may take away your own breath. Initially. But it will
give you back your soul.

Be affirmed by those early words of Genesis, "Whatever he named it...it was."[20]

~ *Naming acts of kindness.* The editors of Conari
Press (now an imprint of Red Wheel/Weiser) created
quite a sensation when they used the phrase "random
acts of kindness" as the title of a book, and it became a
bestseller by that name.[21] When country music legend
June Carter Cash died in May 2003, the family initially
planned a private funeral, but they were overruled by
Johnny Cash. So on a sunny spring day, fifteen hundred people — songwriters, devoted fans, movie stars,
friends, family, and, of course, gawkers — came to her
funeral.

After a musical tribute with Sheryl Crow, the Oak
Ridge Boys, the Gatlin Brothers, Emmylou Harris, and
members of the Cash family and road show, there was
a time to celebrate June Carter Cash's kindnesses.
Like the time she sent a fur coat to be auctioned by
the Lafayette, Tennessee, Rotary Club. Or the time her
stepdaughter overheard "the nicest conversation" for
a half-hour and wondered who June was talking to. "I
said, 'June, who was it?'" June Carter Cash replied,
"Well, honey, it was a wrong number."[22]

Name your grief. Name the kindnesses and the hard-ships with your dead. Tell the truth. Tell God. Tell whoever will listen.

On the long journey to a far place, give yourself permission to name your losses.

You Have Permission
to Reinvent Yourself

As always happens in life, something was coming
to an end and something new was beginning.
— Eleanor Roosevelt, reflecting on widowhood[1]

Two couples had played cards for years. Now a young
widow, her husband dead less than a month, enter-
tained their friends alone. The weekend was packed
with painful reminders of what once had been and what
would never again be. Repeatedly she asked: How do I
build a me without him in a world where I wanted only
an us? Words failed the normally articulate guests. In
an effort to cheer up the widow, one said, "Look, you're
young. You will marry again. You may even have more
children."

The words stunned her. How dare they say such
things! She had a reputation for being gracious, and she
listened as they spun a potential future for her.

The next week, the widow sent a thank-you note for
the gifts they had brought her children. Having had time
to ponder their words she also wrote, "You must know
that I consider my life to be over. And I will spend the
rest of my life waiting for it really to be over."[2]

Rather a harsh assessment from a thirty-four-year-
old. Yet she felt her time in the limelight was over;
she would now place her attention on her two children.
Jackie Kennedy's words, in December 1963, have been

reiterated by many grievers. Jackie once confided in Billy Baldwin, a decorator, "Can anyone possibly understand how it is to have lived in the White House, and then suddenly be living alone as the President's widow?"[3] First Ladies whose husbands are completing a term have the time and resources to plan the transition to life after the White House; presidential widows do not. Moreover, gawkers and paparazzi wanting glimpses of Caroline and John Jr. constantly surrounded Mrs. Kennedy's temporary lodging in Georgetown.

~ *An end to widowhood.* In time, Jackie Kennedy discovered her strength, as many widows and widowers do, when she announced her decision to marry Greek tycoon Aristotle Onassis in 1968. (Francis Cleveland had been the only presidential widow to remarry; she married Thomas Jex Preston Jr. five years after the president's death in 1908.) Jackie's decision created a media frenzy.

The assassinations in 1968 of Martin Luther King and her brother-in-law Robert Kennedy — the children's surrogate father — prodded Jackie, who feared for the safety of her children. "I wanted to get away. They were killing Kennedys and I didn't want them to harm my children."[4] Onassis's fortune offered isolation and safety.

Millions asked how she could abandon her grief for the fallen president. Others questioned how she could abandon her faith. By marrying the divorced Onassis, she risked excommunication from the Roman Catholic Church. Overnight, "The martyred heroine of Camelot's ...image was shattered."[5] Sure some people wanted her to move on, but not that far. The halo around

Jackie's head was tarnished. However, many people insisted that Jackie was entitled to happiness wherever she could find it.

The public was equally stunned when Jackie Kennedy Onassis moved back to New York, separating from Onassis. Jackie was not at his side when he died in March 1975. Jackie reinvented herself again, not with a new husband, but with a new job. She worked as an editor at Viking and then moved to Doubleday, editing an average of a dozen books each year until shortly before she died in 1994.[6]

~ *Understanding a loss within a social network.* Adjustment to loss, according to Robert Neimeyer, "can only be understood in the broader social context" of the griever's relationships.[7] Unfortunately, many grief theories, therapies, and support groups ignore the broader social network in which the individual grieves. If John Donne was right that "No man is an island . . . every man is a piece of the continent," then an individual's grief has widespread implications. Neimeyer estimated that a death impacted the lives of 128 individuals. "With this in mind, it is more accurate to see ourselves as participants in a grief system, rather than as isolated individuals affected by a loss."[8]

Imagine three interlocking rings, like those in the Olympic icon. These rings represent yourself, your family, and the broader society. Grief work goes on in all three rings simultaneously.

~ *The self must come first.* Grief first has to be honored within the framework of oneself, along the quiet canyons and corridors of hearts and memories. Not unlike the safety instructions on airplanes that direct adults to put on their oxygen mask and then help their children, you must attend to your own grief first. Eleanor Roosevelt's life may help us understand the three-rings concept. Mrs. Roosevelt's grief, following the death of her husband, Franklin Roosevelt, in 1945, was layered upon her previous experiences.

As an eight-year-old child, teased about being the ugly duckling of the family, Eleanor saw her world change when her twenty-nine-year-old mother, a society leader in New York, died unexpectedly in 1892 of diphtheria. Anna Hall Roosevelt's will stipulated that the children should not live with their father. Eleanor dearly loved her father, Elliott, an alcoholic who had been separated from Anna. Visits with her father were rare because her grandmother, Valentine Hall, refused to allow their father to see the children without her supervision. So Eleanor cherished his letters. Eleanor had created something of a fantasy relationship to accommodate his prolonged absences.

A year later, when Eleanor's seven-year-old brother Elliott died of diphtheria, Eleanor sank "into a deepening sense of abandonment and loneliness." Her father wrote her, "We bury little Ellie tomorrow up at Tivoli by Mother's side. He is happy in Heaven with her, so now you must not grieve or sorrow."[9] Thus, the adored father constricted Eleanor's loss: "so now you must not grieve."

In August 1894, Elliott Roosevelt died at age thirty-four. Grandmother Hall did not allow Eleanor and Hall, the younger son, to attend the funeral. Eleanor's grandson later disclosed, "There was no closure provided, and none allowed."[10] Three traumatic deaths in less than twenty-four months permanently challenged Eleanor's capacity to trust and to love.

For the next eleven years, "The powerful feelings Elliott elicited in his young daughter of powerful but ultimately tragic and flawed love would remain shut down in her heart"[11] until awakened in a relationship with Franklin.

In 1909, Eleanor was devastated by the death of Franklin Jr., eight months old, due to influenza and pneumonia. She faulted herself for turning over responsibility for the children to nannies, although that was the custom among the wealthy. Losing both her parents, a brother, and a son by age twenty-five was a heavy emotional burden.

She became pregnant again immediately. Her grandson observed, "The deep sorrow she felt at the death of her baby boy had reawakened the melancholy of her relationship with her own father." Not surprisingly, Eleanor named the new baby Elliott after her father.[12]

Then Franklin Roosevelt developed polio. Eleanor rose to the occasion and supported his political ambitions by becoming his legs and ears while he was governor of New York and during their twelve years in the White House. Few Americans knew that Franklin Roosevelt could not walk.

~ *Reviewing a life.* Franklin died on April 12, 1945. To her dismay, Eleanor learned that his affair with her former social secretary, Lucy Mercer, had not ended in 1918 when she discovered it, but had continued up to, literally, the day of his death. Though they had never been as close after her discovery of the affair, she had assumed an honesty between them.

Eleanor realized the complicity of her daughter, Anna, and of the Secret Service agents who, in the twelve Roosevelt years in the White House, had become like family.

Her grandson David observed: "She was faced with beginning her life anew as widow of a president, with tremendous uncertainty and not a little bitterness. Thus, whenever asked of her feelings about that time, her answer would be one of almost impersonal detachment. His death was a 'terrible blow' but not a 'personal sorrow.' It was all the more a sadness felt by 'all those to whom this man who now lay dead, and who happened to be my husband, had been a symbol of strength and fortitude.'"[13]

Her train trip with the body from Warm Springs, Georgia, to Washington, D.C., gave her time to formulate a strategy for life after the limelight she had cherished as First Lady: "I lay in my berth all night with the window shade up, looking out at the countryside he had loved and watching the faces of the people at stations, and even at the crossroads, who came to pay their last tribute all through the night."[14]

~ *Revisiting assumptions.* Some grievers relinquish deeply held assumptions. Many have never thought death, particularly a violent death, could touch them. One widower told me, "I just always assumed that I would go first. We never talked about me outliving her."

Grievers have had to relinquish the assumption that people who promised to support them and be there for them would come through. One daughter told me that she flew home after her father's funeral grateful for the large turnout of friends for the visitation and funeral. "Mom will have lots of support. I lost track of the individuals who said, 'Just let us know if there is anything we can do for your mother.' I soon discovered those words are just a cliché mumbled in funeral homes."

Eleanor Roosevelt was not the only widow to learn of a husband's infidelity at the time of or after a death. One widow told me that her husband's girlfriend came to the visitation, walked up, and said confidently, "We will need to talk."

"About what?!"

"About me getting the things I know he would want me to have."

The widow leaned forward and spoke as she never had before: "Over my dead body! Get the hell out of here. Now!" Unfortunately, I do not know how that story ended; at the time of the telling, it was still a work in progress.

Some grievers have assumed a will or adequate life insurance would provide for them financially. Some have assumed certain properties were fully paid for. Some have assumed that heirs would not fight over stuff — "Not our family!" Some have assumed that the children from previous marriages would not be a problem.

A shrill "This cannot be happening to me!" does little to negate the unfolding realities after a death. Thus, some grief keepers have to juggle their grief over the death of a loved one with their grief over the loss of their previously safe assumptive world.

〰 *A time of transition.* Death forces survivors to reinvent themselves, sometimes immediately. Grief feels something like being "between trapezes," when, as Marilyn Ferguson notes, "There's nothing to hold on to."[15] Candice Carpenter described this transition as "between chapters." "You're not who you were, you're not yet who you are becoming."[16]

Robert Lincoln had to redefine himself after his father's death. As the oldest son, this army officer became head of the family. Even before his father died, he tried to ease his mother's distress. As his father lay dying, Robert tried to calm her: "Mother, please put your trust in God and all will be well." Finally, because of her hysteria, Secretary of State Steward had her removed from the room.[17]

Robert learned that "a President who dies in office remains the property of the public until he is accorded the last rites, and his family is forced to share their dead with the nation."[18] Robert immediately faced a conflict over where the president should be buried. He assumed Springfield, the family home before the presidency, but Mrs. Lincoln preferred Chicago. Once Springfield was chosen, a site in Springfield had to be determined. Robert promptly resigned his army commission in order to care for his mother and his brother, Tad. Two weeks after the assassination, Robert wrote President Andrew Johnson, "My mother is so prostrate that I must beg your indulgence.... Mother tells me that she cannot possibly be ready to leave here for 2½ weeks." (Six weeks would pass before she left the White House.) Eventually, Robert would institutionalize his mother and be estranged from her.

As difficult as handling the details of his father's death, Tad's death in 1871, and his mother's death in 1882, while Robert was minister to England he faced what he called "the hardest of many hard things" when his son, Abraham "Jack" Lincoln II, died at age sixteen in 1890. Robert had dreamed that this son would some-day take a place in his grandfather's law firm, Isham, Lincoln, and Beale. Lincoln, like many grievers, had not appreciated the extent of his expectations for his son. "I did not realize until he was gone how deeply my thoughts of the future were in him."[19]

What went through his mind that November 1890 day as he watched his son's casket placed in the pres-idential vault with his grandparents and three uncles? Robert could never escape the fact that he was the son of Abraham Lincoln. After his death in 1926, the *New York Herald Tribune* editorialized him: "Robert T. Lin-coln did not live in the shadow of his father's greatness. He carved out a career for himself, mostly apart from the controversies of politics."[20]

~ *Reinventing Eleanor.* Technically, she ceased being the First Lady with her husband's death. America had a new First Lady, Bess Truman. In a sense, Eleanor would be First Lady in people's hearts, at least until the presi-dent's burial in Hyde Park. Roosevelt had put his funeral wishes in writing. Both Eleanor and Franklin intensely disliked the practice of viewing a corpse in an open cas-ket. "We had made up our minds that we would never allow it."[21]

Since services were to be held in the White House, the casket was placed in the East Room and opened long enough for Eleanor to place flowers inside. The casket was not reopened, despite persistent requests by the Russian ambassador to view the corpse. Josef Stalin wanted assurance that Roosevelt had not been poisoned.[22] Eleanor recalled, "It seemed to me that everyone in the world was in the East Room for the funeral services except three of my own sons."[23] They were serving in the military and could not return in time for the services.

It's one thing to lose a husband. It is another thing to lose a husband who is president of the United States during a war. Eleanor had to grieve in the context of her family — now complicated by her estrangement with her daughter, Anna — and the sorrowing American public.

Over time, further revelations would challenge the public's image of FDR. Eleanor may not have suspected the relationship between FDR and Margaret "Daisy" Suckley, his cousin and confidante. After Suckley's death the letters between the two were made public. More than one "other woman" had competed in the president's complicated emotional life.[24]

~ *What do I want to do now?* Like all grievers, as a widow Eleanor Roosevelt had to ponder the question: Who am I now? How do I define my identity? What do I want to do with the life I have left? Moreover, Eleanor had a relationship with the loyal readers of her syndicated newspaper column, "My Day." She took off only four days from writing her column.

She also had been a force to be reckoned with in the Democratic Party. Until her death, she continued to wield great influence on candidates and public issues. Anyone who expected Mrs. Roosevelt to join presidential widows Edith Roosevelt, Edith Wilson, and Grace Coolidge to "drift off into obscurity, only to surface for those periodic ceremonial duties expected of former First Ladies"[25] would soon be surprised.

Mrs. Roosevelt immediately made three decisions: "I did not want to run an elaborate household again. I did not want to cease trying to be useful in some way. I did not want to feel old."[26]

The Trumans urged her to take her time in leaving the White House, but Eleanor wanted to leave it as soon as possible. On April 23, eleven days after the president had died, Eleanor left the White House. Immediately the Roosevelt clan gathered at their family home at Hyde Park to settle the estate.[27] One Roosevelt historian commented: "Many a family would have given itself a rest before diving again into the affairs of business of the sensitive issues of inheritance and memorabilia, but not the Roosevelts. Her husband had been an enthusiastic collector of everything historical from miniature books to model boats, and as President he had received scores of gifts from nations and admiring citizens around the world. Assigning presidential and private property to appropriate new homes was a monumental job."[28]

~ *A new you.* In those early days of widowhood, Mrs. Roosevelt "could not have realized that she would survive the shadow cast by her husband," the president, becoming, in her grandson's assessment, "an emancipated woman."[29] She later reflected on her White House years: "On the whole, I think I lived those years very impersonally. It was almost as though I had erected someone outside myself who was the president's wife. I was lost somewhere deep down inside myself. That is the way I felt and worked until I left the White House."[30] Many widows can identify with Mrs. Roosevelt.

Bess Truman, the new First Lady, had a more subdued style, which allowed Mrs. Roosevelt to speak her mind freely. Years before, complaining to FDR about personal attacks on her by newspaper columnists, the president had cautioned her not to get into "pissing contests with a skunk."[31] Now, in the postwar world, soon to be a nuclear world, diplomats would soon gather to organize the United Nations. Mrs. Roosevelt had been expected to promote her husband's commitment to the concept. Truman, determined that the organization should succeed, knew he needed Eleanor's help to influence public opinion. When Truman wanted to appoint her to the U.S. delegation, she asked for time to settle in to her apartment in New York City and deal with some details of the estate, such as turning over the Hyde Park estate to the U.S. government, no small legal transaction. Eventually Truman appointed her and the Senate confirmed her, and she served as an ambassador until Eisenhower was elected. One of her greatest legacies was drafting the Universal Declaration of Human Rights. (She returned to the U.N. in the Kennedy administration.)

~ *Balancing private and public selves.* Grievers balance a private grieving self and a public grieving self. After a period of time, society expects grievers to answer that they are "fine" or respond with brief answers when asked, "How are you doing?" Grievers quickly learn to disclose their true feelings cautiously. Is this person someone to whom I can reveal my vulnerability? Maintaining boundaries, however, can be emotionally and spiritually exhausting for the rookie griever. Some, admittedly, find the "How does she do it?" comments energizing.

Public signs of grief can be especially difficult when grievers are public personalities, politicians, or royalty. Periodically magazine stories examine Princess Diana's sons' adjustments after her death.

172

Marlene Young, president of the National Organization for Victim's Assistance believes that Americans "tend to invest in public figures, more so with media personalities." Many reason that "this person is like me — if I could get to know them." Gerontologist Ken Doka adds, "We identify with points of the biography, for example, with Diana as a young mother rather than a princess."[32]

Some reinvent and reinvest in themselves in the workplace; others, like Coretta Scott King and Candice Lightner, in public causes.

~ *Guarding grief spaces.* Some grievers, particularly those habitualized to caring for others, tell themselves to be strong or be strong for others. Woe is the griever who is deemed weak or grief-challenged or helpless. Walter Brueggemann questioned the denial of grief skills: "The prospect of public grief is a scarce practice in our society, where we are so engaged in self-deception, pretending that everything is 'all right.' Underneath that propaganda, however, we are a deeply troubled community with a great deal of unprocessed hurt."[33]

Mark's Gospel reported Jesus's intentional distancing from his public. "Very early in the morning, while it was still dark, Jesus got up, left the house and went to a solitary place, where he prayed."[34]

That could also be phrased, "went to a solitary place, where he grieved." Mina Edison, the second wife of inventor Thomas Alva Edison, had a solitary place where she withdrew on Sunday afternoons after his death. She had, across the years, asked friends to send stones for a garden at their Fort Myers, Florida, home. As she

walked among the stones, she remembered relationships in a world that must have been far less exciting
after Edison's death.

Many grief keepers find grief space at the cemetery. Asking people whether they go to the cemetery
produces some fascinating discussions. Some quickly
respond: "Why? He's not there!" Others, however, find
cemeteries a safe place to keep their grief. "It's something I do for myself," one grief keeper told me. Some
people find it the only place where they can cry without being interrupted with a proffered tissue or hankie.
During the brief time I lived in a house on cemetery
property in Nashville, I came to recognize the regu-
lars who visited with great punctuality. Some people go
to the cemetery on special occasions like Christmas,
Easter, Valentine's Day, Memorial Day, or a birthday or
anniversary.

I learned about intentionality from the late Henri Nouwen, who urged grievers to have picnics at graves and
to tell stories when visiting the grave. Whenever he went
to Holland, he made his way to a small cemetery in
Geysteren where his mother was buried. Nouwen comments, "When I stand before that simple grave, look at
the cross, and hear the wind play with the leaves of the
tall poplars surrounding the cemetery, I know that I am
not alone. My mother is there, and she speaks to me.
There is no apparition, no mysterious voice, but there
is the simple, inner knowledge that she who died more
than fourteen years ago is still with me."[35]

Nouwen, a priest, taught at Notre Dame, Harvard,
and Yale. His words cannot be easily dismissed as delu-
sional. What does he hear his mother say? "Embraced
by the solitude of the beautiful cemetery, I hear her say

that I must be faithful to my own journey and not be afraid to join her in death someday."[36] In a grief-denying society, grief keepers have to find intentional spaces that are off limits to intruders.

In Phyllis Root's book for children, *The Name Quilt,* Sadie spent her summer vacation with her grandmother. A nightly ritual developed. At bedtime, Grandmother tucked her in with the name quilt. As Sadie traced the names of family members and ancestors with her finger, Grandma told a story about each individual. One day, after washing the quilt and hanging it on the line to dry, the two went fishing. Unexpectedly a windstorm came up. In the fury of the storm, the quilt was blown away. Sadie immediately concluded that all the stories were gone forever. "Hush your crying now," Grandmother comforted the child. "You think I need a quilt to remember? I keep all those names and all of those stories right here inside of me."[37]

Grief keepers keep all the stories inside themselves. Some memories are brought out on special occasions, just as the good china is used to set the table for company.

〜 *Reinvent yourself.* Now what? Eventually grievers finish the details of probating the estate, although for some the process can be long and troublesome. Then many find that they have lots of empty time on their hands. "Keep busy" becomes a temptation, not just an admonition.

John Edwards, a trial lawyer in North Carolina, had a reputation for winning huge settlements in cases involving corporate negligence. He had a good life, a great marriage, and two wonderful children until that

April afternoon in 1996, when Wade, his sixteen-year-old son, died in a one-car accident. Life fell apart for John Edwards. For months, "he and his wife, Elizabeth ...sequestered themselves in their Raleigh house. They still had their fourteen-year-old daughter, Kate, but a cosmic fulcrum had ruptured....his path to success, from mill worker's son to titan of the North Carolina legal community was swift and entirely sensible."[38]

In time, Edwards went back to his legal practice and fell into a busy work routine. Nevertheless, every day began with a visit to the cemetery where he sat on a bench, talked to his son, and prayed. Hours later, he generally was in a courtroom. Death had challenged his fragile assumptions about the predictability of the good life. One day after a friend picked up Edwards and drove him to a state park to show him a path that John and Wade had never jogged, Edwards began running again. "Over time he found daylight, the death of his son less a pounding blow than an existential call to arms — leading him, in a sure if inarticulate way, to a conclusion he and his family, including Wade, had casually discussed for some time: that he should relinquish private life and run for the U.S. Senate."[39]

When Edwards tried to hire Democratic pollster Harrison Hickman to assess his chances, he warned Edwards that he would lose his privacy and hear horrible things said about him in the heat of a political campaign. Hickman put the hard question to the grieving father: "Now, do you still want to run?"

Edwards replied, "Five years ago, that probably would have made a difference to me. But if you've ever had to get up on a table in a medical examiner's office and hug your son good-bye, you know there's nothing they can do to you."[40] A death can help grievers assess what is important to them. In 1998, John Edwards was elected U.S. senator from North Carolina, spurred on in the campaign's tough moments by memories of his son, Wade.

~ *Sharing your grief.* I often close letters, "Take care of you," modifying the common admonition, "Take care." Some grievers, so good at taking care of others, are not careful to take care of themselves. Soon the griever has nothing left to offer others. A key component of keeping a grief is tending your own soul.

Grievers must, from time to time, ponder a question raised by Henri Nouwen, "Are we still in touch with those who have died, or are we living our lives as if those who lived before us never really existed?"[41]

Give yourself permission to grieve. Brothers John and Charles Wesley founded the Methodist Church; John preached and Charles sang. After Charles's death in 1788, it was hard for the patriarch of Methodism to grieve. Soon his preachers began commenting on his absence of feelings, at least as he expressed himself in public. Then came a night at a Bolton meetinghouse; as the congregation sang one of his brother's hymns, he heard these words, "My company before is gone, and I am left alone with thee." John broke into sobs that lasted for some time. Even the head of Methodism had to wonder who he would be without his brother.[42]

Grievers need permission to explore the season "between chapters."

On the long journey to a far place, reinvent yourself.

You Have a Right to Support from Your Family

Today, I asked Brian what emotion or issue he struggles with the most since losing Molly. He didn't have to think long before saying, "That I can't fix it. I can't make everything OK for you, for Matthew and Megan, and for me. I just can't."

—Dawn Siegrist Waltman, *In a Heartbeat*[1]

A young boy in Texas had not been told that his four-year-old sister could die while undergoing treatment for leukemia in New York City. At school one day he looked up and noticed his parents' car enter the parking lot. Good, he thought, they're home — meaning his parents and his sister. He had clearly seen three passengers in the car. Excused by his teacher, he raced to the car but found an empty back seat.

"Where's Robin?" he asked.

"She died."

Suddenly, this boy had questions. He could not understand why his parents had not told him his sister would die. One night at a football game with his dad, the boy grumbled that he wished he was with his sister.

His father, stunned by the comment, asked, "Why do you say that?"

"I bet she can see the game better from up there than we can from here."

While his father was off at the oil fields, this son often served as man of the house, especially afternoons after school when he played inside. His mother explained, "For one who allowed no tears before her death, I fell apart." One day she overheard a neighbor boy invite her son to play at his house. Her son told the friend that although he wanted to, he couldn't. "He couldn't leave his mother. She needed him. That started my cure. I realized I was too much a burden for a little seven-year-old son to carry."[2]

As an adult, George W. Bush recalled that moment in the Sam Houston Elementary School parking lot: "I am certain I saw her, her small head rising above the backseat of my parents' green Oldsmobile." He added, "Forty-six years later, those moments remain the starkest memory of my childhood, a sharp pain in the midst of an otherwise happy blur."[3]

~ **The Lone Ranger grievers.** Some individuals are, or believe themselves to be, lone rangers among their families, churches, and communities. The Lone Ranger, of TV fame, was the sole survivor of the massacre of a troop of Texas Rangers. He put on a mask to hide his true identity and to bring justice following the deaths of his fellow Rangers.

Many grievers must hide their true identities. Many put on masks, ironically, to hide their grief from family. In grief, you discover what your family is really like.

As Susan Ford Wiltshire discovered after her brother's death, some family members are "cordoned off in silence."[4] The cat may not have their tongue, but grief does. Susan offered sage advice, "Sometimes you just have to plow around the stump,"[5] which means plowing around the barriers to a kept grief — even when family members are the stumps.

⁓ *The family can be a lonely place to keep grief.* In many cases, someone selects or is selected to be the de facto manager of the family grief. Many women cannot do their own grieving because they are too busy being strong for others in the family, auditing the grief of family members. A crisis may erupt when the one who has previously managed the family's grief dies.

In some families roles are reversed, and children must care for siblings and run the house while a parent grieves. One mother came home from the hospital and said to her eleven-year-old daughter, "Your brother just died. Take care of your brothers," and then she went to bed for the next six months. In a sense, that young girl's childhood ended that day.

Four-year-old Arthur Ashe, witnessing his father's anguished grief, could not ask questions that might further upset his father, so he buried his questions about his mother's death. "I don't remember grieving over my mother. She died, and life moved on. My father told people how my response to the news, as he sat crying his eyes out between my brother Johnnie and me, was simple enough. 'Don't cry, Daddy,' I consoled him. 'As long as we have each other, we'll be all right.' "

Within twelve months Ashe's beloved grandfather died. Now the six-year-old had two significant losses to face. Later Ashe reflected: "I have understood that this quality of emotional distance in me...may very well have something to do with the early loss of my mother. I have never thought of myself as having been cheated by her death, but I am terribly, insistently, aware of an emptiness in my soul that only she could have filled."[6]

~ *Keeping death's secrets.* Family members are not always equally privy to the facts about a death; in fact, children may be shielded from some raw realities of a death. Some families collude to rewrite the death to make it less harsh and easier to accept. When Joe Kennedy Jr. died in 1944, the family had a hero to mourn (he died on an experimental bombing mission for which he had volunteered). His sister Kick wrote a family friend: "I am a Kennedy. I have a very strong feeling that makes a big difference about how to take things. I saw Daddy and Mother about Joe, and I know we've all got the ability not to be got down."[7]

Four years later, Kick died in a plane crash with her lover in France, and the family again stood strong in public. Only Joe Sr. attended the funeral in London. "Despite his heartache, Joe somehow summoned the presence of mind to shape the public perception of his daughter's death with her married lover. It was important that the story not embarrass the Kennedys and harm the political aspirations of Joe's second son, Jack, who had inherited the mantle of the family standard-bearer.... Though all of London society had been aware of Kick's scandalous affair with [Peter] Fitzwilliam, Joe Kennedy set about fabricating a story that whitewashed his daughter's reputation and became the established version of her death."[8]

Families not in the public eye also spin death narratives. When one ten-year-old's mother died, her father bluntly informed her, "Your mother passed away." As an adult she recounted, "I didn't even know what that meant. And that was the end of the conversation." In a matter of hours all evidence of her mother disappeared from the home. She and her four siblings were not allowed to attend the funeral mass.

Eventually, after a neighbor informed the girl that her mother had died with hepatitis, the child looked up the word in a dictionary. "It said a disease you get through dirty needles. I remember thinking, in a ten-year-old's rationalization and justification, that it was from sewing."[9] When her father became emotionally unavailable for his family, Rosie O'Donnell became chief cook and bottle washer, not just for her siblings but also for a sick grandmother.

~ *Mixing family narrative and fiction.* When a family fictionalizes the story of a family member's death, sooner or later the truth will be discovered. Frances Fonda was hospitalized for depression when Jane and Peter were children. Peter often "prayed to Jesus that he wouldn't let anything bad happen to Mother." After Frances committed suicide in a state sanatorium, a brief service was held at a local funeral home with only two in attendance: Frances's mother, Sophie, and her husband, Henry. What to tell the children? Henry Fonda recalled, "In the car Sophie and I decided that the children were too young for the truth. Sophie suggested that since their mother had been in a hospital for so long, we could just say she got sick and died there."[10] Jane was the first to be told.

"Your mother has died of a heart attack, Jane." The young girl asked to be excused to go to her room. "I sat on the edge of the bed and wondered why I couldn't cry. And I thought, 'How weird. I'm never going to see her again, and I can't cry.' I never cried."[11]

Fonda was more guarded in telling his son. "Peter, Mummy is dead." Peter began crying. Hours later,

Henry Fonda hugged his children, wiped Peter's tears, and drove into New York City. Leland Hayward, the director of the play Fonda was appearing in, ordered the cast, "Behave just as if nothing has happened. He's here and he wants to do his job and he wants to work."[12] After all, on Broadway the show must go on. That night, a young boy cried himself to sleep. Peter recalled, "It was Friday, April 14, Jesus had failed me. Jesus had let me down. Jesus forgot my prayer about Mother. I was too young to know that little in life was fair. . . . I never asked Jesus for anything again."[13] It would take years before Peter Fonda discovered how his mother had died, and before he could forgive his mother for dying and his grandmother and his father for their deception.

In some families, particularly when death is stigmatized, family members collude to avoid keeping the grief and to keep the cause or circumstances of the death secret, at least from certain family members. Many young adult males died in the early days of the AIDS epidemic, their sexual orientation and diagnosis hidden from brothers, sisters, nieces, nephews, grandparents, and, in a few cases, spouses. In the midst of so much death, Peter Selwyn, an AIDS specialist at Yale University, began to revisit his own narrative. Selwyn was eighteen months old when his father died from a fall from an office window. "Confronted with the deaths of all these young men and women . . . I began to realize that I had never come to terms with this first and primal loss."[14] "Because of the unusual circumstances of his death, this event and even the memory of his life quickly became family secrets that I was not permitted to discuss, so in effect, I experienced a double loss. In some ways, I had come to believe that he had never even existed. It is perhaps a testimony to the many layers of denial and avoidance with which my family — and I myself — had covered up his death, that it wasn't until six years into the AIDS epidemic that I ever connected my work with any conscious thoughts about my father."[15]

Immersed in death and grief and parenting two young children, Selwyn supported his grief for patients by attending wakes and funerals — something other specialists refused to do. He began deconstructing the narrative, discovering many gaping holes until a starker truth stalked him: perhaps his father had not fallen accidentally. "Whenever I asked, which was not very often, I was told that he had died in a fall from a window, that he had had poor balance, and that this was a terrible accident. I suppose that this seemed so bizarre that maybe I believed it was true; or else, given the way people's expressions and tones of voice would change whenever I brought it up, I got the message that this was not something that was acceptable to discuss. My mother would use an awkward, slightly disapproving tone when she used the phrase 'your father,' which was the only way I ever heard her refer to him."[16]

Moreover, there were no photos, no letters, no mementos, nothing to remind a boy of an unknown father. Peter conceded, "It is too easy to blame her for not keeping his memory alive." However, "she did what she had to do: she stayed, and she survived." At least, he concluded, "my mother did not let what must have been her own deep rage tarnish any of her feelings toward me." Years later, he wrote, "I wish somehow that she could have let me share in some of the pain rather than trying to shield it from me."[17]

Adults do children no lasting favors by masking the truth; sooner or later the truth will be told, whether accidentally or as part of coming of age. Eventually, when Selwyn asked his mother whether she had kept any of his father's personal effects, she retrieved items from a shoebox in the closet: his father's glasses, his wedding ring, and a wallet containing his driver's license, a W-2 tax slip, and his Selective Service card. "I still have these few items in a wooden box at home, and I am thankful to have some small tokens of remembrance. But mostly, if I stop to think about it, I feel cheated and sad, like I deserved to have more of him."[18]

~ *When family loyalties compete for your grief.* Few First Ladies have been as impacted by grief as Mary Todd Lincoln. As the wife of an Illinois attorney, she grieved for her three-year-old son, Edward Baker Lincoln, who died in 1850. As First Lady she was devastated when another son, William Wallace "Willie" Lincoln, died in the White House at age eleven on February 20, 1862. Biographer Doug Wead concluded that while that death "pushed First Lady Mary Lincoln over the emotional edge," it "refined the president's ability to empathize with the nation's suffering as many lost sons during the Civil War."[19] Both parents lost the same sons, but they grieved differently. After Willie was embalmed, Mrs. Lincoln visited the Green Room long enough to place a sprig of laurel on his chest. She did not attend the funeral — the custom in that day was to protect "the delicate sex" — and in her remaining years in the White House, she never again entered the Green Room.

Many know of Willie's death and the president's assassination. But Mrs. Lincoln juggled other family griefs, including her brother's death when she was three and her mother's death when she was six. Eight of her half-brothers were Confederates, a detail that did not go unnoticed by critics who accused Mrs. Lincoln of being a Southern sympathizer. Two months after Willie's death, her brother Sam died at the Battle of Shiloh. Brother David died at the battle of Vicksburg in 1863. Later that fall, the family favorite, Aleck, died in a skirmish near Baton Rouge. Upon receiving word of Aleck's death, Mrs. Lincoln cried, "Oh little Aleck, why had you to die?"[20]

Washington insiders knew about the "Willie raisers," or séances, in the White House. Mrs. Lincoln defended the séances, assuring Senator Charles Sumner, "a very slight veil separates us from the loved and lost and to me there is comfort in the thought that though unseen by us they are very near."[21] She wrote her sister Emilie, "Willie lives. He comes to me every night and stands at the foot of the bed with the same sweet adorable smile he always has had. He does not always come alone. Little Eddie is sometimes with him."

Although Mary Todd Lincoln became emotional when informed of her half-brothers' deaths, she "would not grieve for traitors," she declared to her friend Elizabeth Keckly, "even if they were relatives."[22] "He [Aleck] made his choice long ago. He decided against my husband, through him against me. He has been fighting against us and since he chose to be our deadly enemy, I see no special reason why I should bitterly mourn his death."[23]

Apparently, many nights when her sons returned from the spirit world, Aleck tagged along, which must have created interesting nocturnal moments.

After Mary's brother-in-law, General Benjamin Hardin Helm, was killed at Chattanooga, the president arranged special pass for his widow, Emilie, to visit the White House in December 1863. The sisters had not seen each other since the outbreak of hostilities. Mary was horrified that her favorite half-sister "overnight had been transformed from a gay almond-eyed belle . . . into a bitter, grief-sotted widow."[24] Initially the sisters comforted each other, avoiding any discussion of the war. That may have been possible within the family circle but not at social events. After one exchange with Emilie, General Dan Sickles angrily demanded of Lincoln how he could tolerate "that rebel in your house."[25]

In the fall of 1864, Emilie returned to Washington to seek a permit to sell six hundred bales of cotton. Lincoln would not accommodate his sister-in-law unless she took an oath of loyalty to the United States. Emilie left the White House enraged. In a letter she accused him of being unsympathetic to her needs as a widow and blaming him for the deaths of her husband and her brother, Levi. She ended the letter: " . . . your bullets have made us what we are."[26] In retaliation, Mary never saw or corresponded with her sister again.

〜 *Personal grief history.* In order to understand someone's grief for a particular person, one must know that person's previous experience with loss. A recent death may reboot a grief that has been mothballed. Lisa Beamer discovered this after her husband died on Flight 93 on September 11, 2001. Her experience as a widow with three children was shaped by having watched, at age fifteen, her mother as a widow with four children. She recalled: "In the midst of her own pain, Mom stepped up and did her best to maintain some

187

sense of normalcy in our lives. She didn't have hours to sit and cry; she had four kids to care for. Consequently, she didn't take a lot of time to grieve; she plunged right back into the daily grind. Years later she admitted, 'I'm not sure I handled it the best way.' But at the time, that was the only choice that made any sense to her."[27]

The times Lisa's mother did express her grief were difficult for teenaged Lisa. "It was too difficult for me to bear my own grief and empathize with Mom at the same time." So, "We got to the place where we hid our pain from each other, but it was always there, right below the surface."[28] With only a small pension, Lisa's mother had to juggle going to work with raising four children. "Watching Mom deal with the financial stress created by Dad's untimely death left an indelible impression on me. I told myself, I never want to be in that vulnerable position. . . . That is a mistake I vowed never to make. I knew firsthand how unexpected life's events can be. I wanted to hope for the best but plan for the worst."[29]

At age thirty-two, Lisa Beamer found herself in her mother's shoes.

 ~ *Balancing multiple losses.* In April 1968, three small children playing in front of a television set heard, "We bring you this special bulletin: Dr. Martin Luther King Jr. has been shot in Memphis." One of those children, Dexter, remembered, "Martin [my brother] and I looked at each other. We said nothing." The boys ran into their parents' bedroom, where Coretta Scott King was talking on the phone with Jesse Jackson at the hospital. When their sister Yolanda entered the bedroom, she pressed her hands over her ears and screamed, "Don't tell me! Don't tell me!" and ran from the bedroom. Mrs. King, who had long feared this day, realized she had to talk to her sons. "Pain filled Mother's face. She encircled us boys in her arms and drew in a deep breath, as if about to dive underwater. 'Your father — there's been an accident.' From then on our mother was stoic. She made you feel that she was in control. No hysterics."[30]

The home filled with friends trying to comfort the King family. When one family friend became hysterical, Dexter concluded that his father had died. "I knew when Mrs. Ward fell back. As a seven-year-old I didn't have an understanding of death, but I knew it was worse than the first report: he had been shot, he had lived. Now the worst had happened."[31]

Other kids whose fathers are killed — and that is no small number in the course of a year — can grieve in private, but not if their father was the Reverend Doctor Martin Luther King Jr. As a result of the media focus, at the funeral, Dexter recalled, "I tried not to feel. I watched Bernice instead. . . . I never cried over my father's death. I watched Mother and took clues from her. I never saw her seem agitated or disturbed. She knew how closely the four of us watched her. If she'd gone to pieces . . . But she didn't. I thought that was the way you were supposed to act. That was the first death really close I'd been exposed to."[32]

At nighttime, however, in Dexter's dreams, his father was still alive. Dexter recalled, "I was happy." But when he woke up, the raw reality announced its presence anew.

The King children were blessed to have many surrogate father figures like Granddaddy King, Uncle A. D. (A. D. Williams King, Martin's brother), Uncle Andy (Andrew Young), and Uncle Harry (Belafonte). Still, Mrs. King told Martin III that he was head of the house

now, which Martin took to heart, creating tensions between the three older children, "with him suddenly
trying to be the man, with no model." What was it like
for Mrs. King? "Her stoical demeanor didn't change. But
now roles were shifting in the sense that she now became the central figure. Almost the first thing she did
was germinate the idea for the King Center. She transferred her grieving into work, then immersed herself
in that."[33]

Once Martin III told his mother that "he wished he had
two mothers, one who did the work my father wanted
done, and one who stayed home and was a mother."
Dexter recalled, "Mother was torn. We'd lost our leader,
yet this man who had become our martyr had told us to
keep moving."

What the King children experienced is common. A
widowed mother often has to work. Few get the lux-
ury of grieving full-time. Dexter reflected back on the
choices his mother faced: "It was only much later that I
ever began to understand a little bit of what my mother
must have gone through. She was a beautiful, gifted
wife, a mother of four small children, and a partner
whose life course was suddenly, shockingly changed
forever in an instant. She obviously had to find a way to
personally make sense of her tragedy, to find her own
personal peace."[34]

Fifteen months later, the King children were stunned
when Uncle A. D. drowned in his backyard swimming
pool, days after taking the King children on a vacation
to Jamaica — a death some family members did not
believe was accidental.

Again the Kings gathered in historic Ebenezer Baptist Church for a funeral. "Outside Atlanta, Uncle A. D.'s

untimely death barely caused a ripple of attention. But inside our family, it was a nightmare."[35] Dexter summarized this compounding loss, "We had to keep on living — that much was not open to speculation, theorizing, or wondering why. We had to keep on living, keep forging on."[36]

Less than five years later, tragedy struck again when Dexter's maternal grandmother, Alberta Williams "Big Mama" King, was killed by a deranged gunman as she played the organ during a Sunday morning service.

In a hospital emergency room, the King grandchildren gathered and said their good-byes. "It was sad. But I didn't cry," Dexter recalled. Dexter told no one that he felt partially responsible because he and some friends had snuck out of the service to buy candy at a convenience store nearby. "If I'd been there, maybe I could have done something."[37]

Bernice King voiced her anxiety: "If you're not safe in church, where are you safe? If you can't go to church and not worry about getting killed, where can you go?"[38] For months, the youngest King child would flip through the family photo albums, asking, "I wonder who's next?"

~ *Divorce colors grief.* Postdivorce issues pollute grief when a family member dies. Norma Zimmer sang on Lawrence Welk's television show for years. Although her parents had divorced, Norma was attempting to build a relationship with her father. After he was found dead in his car in a grocery store parking lot, Norma broke the news to her mother.

"Mother accepted the news without a trace of emotion. No tears, no trembling of the jaw. She did say, 'What a shame he had to die like that.' I felt she was glad he was out of her life." She attended the funeral reluctantly to support Norma. "I tried to hold back the tears," Norma recalled, "because I knew if I started to sob I wouldn't be able to stop. When a few tears squeezed past my swollen lids and trickled down my cheeks, Mother leaned over and whispered to me, 'I should have brought a towel,' referring to the many times she had gone into her bathroom to get me a towel when she knew I was going to cry. Then she would toss it in my lap and say, 'Now cry.' "[39] With just a few simple words, Norma's mother downplayed her daughter's grief.

~ **When spouses grieve independently.** Nothing challenges a marriage like the death of a child, regardless of the child's age, especially if it is an only child. One mother described such early bereaving: "I lay across the bed sobbing at the rawness of my pain. It hurt so much. Mingled in with the grief was a stab of bitterness as I listened to the buzz of my husband's power tools. Three days earlier our baby had died. Three days! So why was he 'up and at 'em' as if nothing had happened? Where were the signs of his pain and his grief? Didn't he understand what we had lost?"[40]

Tensions develop following the death of a child when one parent wants to keep the grief and the other wants to move on (or is perceived to be moving on). Statistics about the divorce risk after a child's death are often dumped on grieving couples. "It is commonly assumed that the death of a child serves also as a death knell to the marriage of affected parents." Counselors and clergy often reinforce the threat. "It is unfortunate that, while coping with their grief, parents are all too often presented with the stressful omen that divorce is a fait accompli. It is especially troubling that claims of a high divorce rate are founded on anecdotal speculation and not on empirical evidence."[41]

While their research sample is small, Mark Hardt and Danette Carroll have found a surprisingly low divorce rate. Out of 147 parents, only 11 reported divorcing or separating after the death of a child — 7.5 percent. Admittedly, 29 percent acknowledged that they had thought about divorce or separation. These researchers concluded, "For couples who have lost a child, it is important that divorce does not appear to be the inevitable outcome that has long been assumed."[42]

Mamie Eisenhower, in an interview with *Better Homes and Gardens* in late 1960, observed that "giving up a baby is the hardest trial a young couple may have to face" because it makes a couple different from their peers. Julie Eisenhower wrote that Ikky's death "closed a chapter in the marriage. It could never again be an unblemished love. . . . They now regarded each other with open eyes."[43] Biographer Carlo D'Este added: "Ikky's death left a permanent scar on both parents. Somehow they pretended to cope but fooled no one. Instead of drawing closer together in the wake of Ikky's death, each retreated into a private world of sorrow and suffered in silence, their only common bond their beloved son's death."[44] The temptation that the Eisenhowers succumbed to — immersing themselves in work and isolation — threatens many marriages.

Preexisting factors are critical in the permanence of the marriage. Dawn Siegrist Waltman identified each spouse's willingness to fight for the marriage as critical for the marriage's survivability.[45] Following the death of her daughter, Robin, Barbara Bush returned to Texas ready to move on. She reflected on the initial differences between her husband and herself: "I wanted to get back to real life, but there is a dance that you have to go through to get there. When I wanted to cut out, George made me talk to him, and he shared with me. What a difference that makes. He made me remember that the loss was not just mine. It was his, Georgie's, and Jeb's, our friends' who loved her, and all our family so far away."[46]

For some grieving spouses, marital tension develops because of a competing commitment to keep or jettison the grief. Although strong spousal relationships prior to a child's death may deteriorate, the stronger the marriage before the death the more likely that it will survive. But as one father told me, "The jury can be out for a long time." Assigning guilt or blame for a death, verbalized or assumed, challenges a spousal relationship.

Some grieving parents feel a subtle, even if unspoken, accusation: "Somehow, you must not have been a good enough parent." Paradoxically, each parent must separately grieve a unique relationship with a particular child while also grieving a shared relationship as a couple. Not surprisingly, communication and sexual intimacy can be strained. Some couples feel pressured by family members to abandon their grief and concentrate on having another child. Sex may cease to be comforting and become an obsessive agenda.

~ *Survivor's guilt.* In a culture determined to have grievers move it along, grief has a way of reannouncing its influence in a psychological ambush that gets our attention. Aaron Latham has lived with grief for his sister for years. "I can tell you with certainty that the loss of a sibling leads to survivor guilt. Why her, not me?

194

Wasn't she better than I am? And survivor guilt often leads in turn to callings . . . of one kind or another. A religious calling. A literary calling. A political calling. The calling is strong because you are, in a sense, living for two: You have to do well!"[47]

Some grievers make promises — and some keep the promises. Latham recalled, "As I was leaving the cemetery after my sister's burial thirty-three years ago, I promised: I'm going to write a book — something I had never done — and dedicate it to my sister. Within a year, I had done so."[48]

· Latham went a step further. He devoured books on sibling loss and talked endlessly to psychiatrists. Latham notes that you are bound to revisit the loss as a child when you are an adult. "Actually around forty is when it usually happens. The real bite of survivor guilt clamps down around midlife. Or so I am told. I was forty-nine when it knocked me head over heels. You ask yourself what your sister would think of the use you have made of your life. The life she never had."[49]

Latham noted that George W. Bush's spiritual awakening took place at age thirty-nine. Latham asked Don Evans, the president's trusted friend, whether he thought the loss of his sister had anything to do with Bush's religious awakening. He answered, "Sure. Certainly that's something he thinks about. Your Lord is who you look to in times of pain and suffering." In what Latham terms, "ex post facto suffering."

∽ *The replacement sibling.* Susan Sonnenday Vogel, following the death of her son Mark, feared that her son David would sense a need to become his replacement. She wrote him, "It is my fear that you will believe that you must take Mark's place and your own as well. I fear

195

that you will have to make up for the loss by being more than you are."[50]

When Joseph P. Kennedy Jr. died in World War II, John's life changed; when John's life ended in 1963, Robert's life changed; when Robert's life ended in 1968, Teddy's life changed. Ambassador Joseph Kennedy had planned for Joe to become president and for John to be a historian or academic. Death turned the understudy into the lead.

Joe Kennedy, the patriarch, lamented, "You know how much I had tied my whole life up to his and what great things I saw for him in the future." Young Joseph's death on a bombing mission made him a hero but touched off unresolved feelings in brother Jack. "Now there was no elder brother to compete against, and Joe Jr.'s death sealed his superiority 'forever in his father's heart.'" John complained to family friend Lem Billings, "I'm shadowboxing in a match the shadow is always going to win."[51]

The family should be a natural environment for mutually supported grief. Unfortunately, the family may be the last place to express grief. Of all the materials that I have read in preparation for writing this book, one story still haunts me. Three-year-old Kate became her mother's constant companion following the death of her newborn sister, Ida; her mother was fearful that something would now happen to Kate. For hours, Kate had to sit quietly on her mother's lap in a darkened room as her mother wept. One day while playing in the yard, her uncle invited her to go for a walk.

"No, I mustn't go out of the yard," Kate informed him, "or God'll punish Mamma some more."[52] Three years later, Kate died. The couple was now childless.

Kate's father threw himself into campaigning for a Congressional seat (which he won). I don't know who sat with Kate's mother in the darkened room as she wept this time, but it was not her husband, future president William McKinley.

On the long journey to a far place, look for support within your family.

You Have Permission
to Remember Your Dead

Consciously remembering those who have died is the key that opens our hearts, that allows us to love them in new ways.   —Tom Attig, *The Heart of Grief*[1]

England's King Charles I, on the scaffold, slowly handed the Great George medallion from around his neck to William Juxon, the archbishop of Canterbury. Then he took off his cloak and gave it to Juxon. Before placing his head on the chopping block, he uttered only one word, "Remember."[2]

~ *A culture of forgetters.* A friend observed a conflict between his young son and a neighbor boy on the front porch. His son slammed the door as he walked in the house.

"I am never going to be Michael's friend anymore!" Although my friend chose not to question his son's reaction, that night he was surprised to find the ex-friend sitting beside his son at dinner.

"I thought you were never going to be Michael's friend anymore."

"Dad," his son replied, "I am a good forgetter."

There are lots of good forgetters in contemporary American culture. How quickly we abandon grief and forget our dead. "Forget 'em!" is what many hear when admonished to get over it and move on.

Just before his betrayal, Jesus "took bread, and when he had given thanks, he broke it and said, 'This is my body, which is for you; do this in remembrance of me.'"[3] In thousands of settings around the globe, that verse is used to initiate Eucharist. The phrase "In remembrance of me" has been carved into thousands of communion tables. "Do this" is a command. Jesus was saying: "Remember to remember me!"

∿ *Grief keepers remember creatively and enthusiastically.* Many grievers regret things they failed to do during the life of the deceased. If those grievers fail to remember their loved one, their loss is compounded.

Some people are afraid of dying. Increasingly, given the loss of so many remembrance functions in our society, many individuals are afraid of being deleted, as one would delete a computer file. As a child I played with a Magic Slate by the hour. When I tired of a drawing, I lifted the gray plastic and the image disappeared. That is what some people want to do with their dead. Erase them. While many people are good at promising to remember their loved one, promises have a way of fading.

On the way to speak at a hospice training event in Indiana, I asked the driver to stop at a cemetery in West Lafayette. I had promised my friend John while he was alive — and myself after he died — that I would remember him. At the grave, I poured purple glitter into my hand.

"John, just wanted to drop by for a moment." I tossed glitter into the air over the grave. In the dazzling sunlight the particles drifted downward onto the marker, John Marquis Culver. Later his mother told me: "I knew one of

John's friends had been there because I found glitter on the marker. It pleases me that you remembered John."

A loved one is not gone until two things happen: grief keepers stop saying the name and stop telling stories about the deceased. Admittedly some people find remembering easier when alone or on remembrance-friendly turf. However, when grief keepers do not remember publicly, someone is deprived of a model of remembering.

⁓ **Reduced to pronouns.** Names are the password to memories. Soon after a death, many start using pronouns — he or she — rather than saying the deceased's name. Some people assume that saying the deceased's name deserves a sharp reprimand from Miss Manners. Many assume that saying the name will hurt grievers. Hardly. More grievers are hurt when family and friends stop saying the name of their dead. I nudge group participants who convert to pronouns. "Excuse me, you are pronoun-ing. Please say your loved one's name."

Grief keepers say the name of their deceased any time, any place that they wish. If it makes other people uncomfortable, that is their problem.

⁓ **Remembering actively.** Memories, ads, and commercials ambushed me that first Mother's Day season after my mother died. I remembered gifts I had sent her over the years, time spent choosing just the right card. I could not believe all the reminders for candy, cards, flowers, brunches — seemingly everywhere.

I spent that first Mother's Day afternoon without Mom with fellow grievers at a "Naming of the Names" service. In gathering to honor memories of deceased mothers, the focal symbol was a plain brown grapevine wreath.

When participants registered, Rhonda Monke, the facilitator, calligraphed the names of their mothers on ribbons attached to a nosegay. During the service, participants walked to a microphone, said their mothers' name, and related one characteristic about her they would always remember. Individuals then attached the ribbon to the wreath. By the end of their service that plain wreath was stunningly beautiful.

Trying out this new regimen of grief, I listened closely to the words of my co-grievers. One young adult's voice quivered as he said his mother's name and whispered, "My mother loved me." When he began to sob, no one looked away. I also watched confident professionals gulp and try to force memories across their lips. In emotion-heavy voices, memories got loose. The emotions could have been limited by marching forward and attaching the ribbons without saying the names, but something remarkable happened in that space when particular mothers were named: Mary, Louise, Margaret, Anne, Betty, Mabel, Florence, Joelina. Many grievers found that service of remembrance a brief safe place to remember.

~ *Remembering accurately.* "Speak no ill of the dead" is one of the most disenfranchising admonitions in the English language. In too many families, active remembering is stymied by a collusion to stick to an acceptable script or an official version of a life.

One man struggled at his best friend's funeral. The friend's father — long in denial about his son's sexual orientation — jabbed his finger into the friend's chest. "Now let's get one thing straight; I don't want any damn gay stuff going on around here! Tell your friends I will personally throw them out of this funeral home if they try anything!"

At the funeral, the family sat in the front of the chapel. Gay friends sat in the back. Acceptable friends, i.e., straight friends, sat between the two groups. No mention was made of the deceased's involvement in raising funds for various AIDS projects or singing in the Gay Men's Chorus. No acknowledgment was made of the friend who had so faithfully cared for the deceased man until almost the moment of his death, when the family, finally, had shown up and immediately asked the friend to leave. "This is a time for family." When the friend protested, the father threatened, "Don't make me call security!" This friend's grief was ignored as he stood in the hall while his friend died in the bosom of the family that had estranged him.

~ *The tradition of* **hesped.** Grief in the Jewish faith is influenced by the tradition of *hesped,* a desire for a balanced eulogy. Anne Brener explained, "A *hesped* should accurately represent the life of the deceased. It is as inappropriate to laud an evil person as to malign a good one."[4] Orthodox Jews may warn: "Cursed be anyone who says 'Amen' to a false eulogy."

My mother often challenged me. "If you can't say something good about a person, best not say anything." From the eulogy scripts I hear, other mothers must have passed on that admonition too. Eulogies invariably concentrate on the positive deeds or characteristics of the deceased. When a balanced narrative is not presented, "People close to the deceased often complain that the person described in the *hesped* was not the person they knew. Those who knew the whole person may mourn burdened with secrets."[5] No few persons leave a funeral or memorial service disappointed, irritated, or angry because someone did not remember the deceased as thoroughly as listeners wished.

Funeral director Robert Vanderbergh recalled a funeral mass that was proceeding smoothly with a succession of glowing eulogies. Then a man jumped up and shouted, "Let's stop joking. He was a no-good son of a bitch!" The requiem mass was concluded immediately.[6]

For some, the success of a funeral requires that everyone stick to the script. Some individuals are denied opportunities to speak because the family fears that what they might say would fall outside their desired window of remembrance; some families have narrow windows.

In their book *Liberating Losses,* Jennifer Elison and Chris McGonigle describe a widow who "sat through the services with her own memories," which she could not reconcile with the public memories. Her husband had been something of a Dr. Jekyll and Mr. Hyde. Few mourners knew that when she and the minister checked out her husband's office, they discovered computer files of gay pornography. In that moment of discovery the widow realized why her husband seldom initiated sex and why he spent so much time at night "at the office." In the mathematics of grief, two and two equaled more than an unpleasant four! At the services she felt as if she were mourning a different Nick from the rest of the world. She heard her husband described as "intense," a man who "told it like it was," but that was as close as anyone got to her reality. His brother and parents knew about the abuse but never referred to it. Nick's aunt advised her to "just forget about all the bad things about Nick and grieve for the loss of the good."[7]

Some eulogists resort to verbal gymnastics to tip the scales of memory to the positive side. A friend conducting a service was stunned, after a glowing fictitious eulogy, when the widow said to a daughter in a stage whisper, "Good thing he didn't have to live with him!"

In some families secrets lay strewn across the memory's terrain like land mines. And there's nothing like a funeral to unleash secrets. Some people discover they were not the only one that the deceased had abused, lied to, or manipulated. No few sexually abused daughters or emotionally abused sons have sat through visitations, funerals, and memorial services fighting to go along with the desired script.

Few can keep grief and collude with scripts that do not accurately reflect the life of the deceased or their relationship with the deceased. Real memories intrude and demand acknowledgment. Some grievers need a private *hesped.* In the Christian tradition, some people find support in Jesus's promise, "For where two or three are gathered together in my name, there am I with them."[8] Grief keepers intentionally create safe spaces to honor their particular memories of the deceased.

~ **When "loved one" is not appropriate.** Elison and McGonigle charge that the phrase "loved one" compounds the issue when the deceased were not loved. One chaplain arrived in an emergency room to console a new widow. Without hearing any of the family narrative, the chaplain volunteered, "I am sure you will be comforted by all the warm memories of your loved one."

"Loved one!" the widow snapped. "Honey, these are tears of joy. I am glad this bastard is dead! The quicker we can get him in the ground, the better!" Nothing in clinical pastoral education had prepared the chaplain for this widow's reality.

Several of us listened to a young man rant after he discovered that he and his brothers were not acknowledged in their father's will despite promises that the will would make up for years of financial and emotional neglect. Someone spoke up. "You are going to have to live with a very unpleasant reality: Your father was a son of a bitch while he was alive and he is one sorrier son of a bitch dead!" That observation sucked the pretense out of the room.

Remembrance can be difficult for siblings who share the same parent biologically but not emotionally. Some grieve with the pained reality that a sibling was a parent's favorite.

One woman explained, "My relationship with my dad ended years ago over a report card. I was a C student. My dad humiliated me: 'Why can't you be like your sisters? They get As.' I decided to work hard. I did extra credit. I stayed after school. And it paid off. I had the best report card ever: two As and three B+s. I couldn't wait for my dad to see my report card. When he came in from work, I ran screaming, 'Daddy, look at my report card.' He glanced at it and snarled, 'You must have cheated. That's the only way you could get As.' I was crushed. After that, we tolerated each other. At his funeral, I grieved not for the father in the casket but for the father I wished I had had. My dad died a long, long time ago."

Therese Rando insisted that extreme anger or extreme guilt distorts grief.[9] Anger also distorts how we remember the deceased. Some grievers remember selectively. Elison and McGonigle describe one widows' rage: "I wanted to go out to the cemetery, dig him up, and kill him all over again."[10]

~ ***Remembering with regret.*** Some grievers are angry at themselves, at perceived deficiencies as caregivers, lamenting that they could have, should have done more. Eighteen-month-old Langdon Clemens, Mark Twain's son, died on June 2, 1872. Thirty-four years later, near the end of his long career as a humorist, in a rare reference to his son, Twain confessed his assumed responsibility for the child's death. "His mother trusted him to my care and I took him [for] a long drive in an open barouche for an airing. It was a raw, cold morning, but he was well wrapped about with furs and, in the hands of a careful person, no harm would have come to him. But I soon dropped into a reverie and forgot all about my charge. The furs fell away and exposed his bare legs. By and by the coachman noticed this, and I arranged the wraps again, but it was too late. The child was almost frozen. I hurried home with him. I was aghast at what I had done, and feared the consequences."[11]

Few who laughed at Twain's humor knew of the regret that clogged his memories. The humorist who had charmed millions concluded, "I have always felt shame for that treacherous morning's work and have not allowed myself to think of it when I could help it." He added, "I doubt if I had the courage to make the confession at that time. I think it most likely that I have never confessed until now."[12] Although Langdon Clemens died of diphtheria, Twain blamed himself.

~ ***Remembering aggressively.*** As a child I faithfully watched the television series *I Remember Mama,* portraying the experiences of a Norwegian family that had migrated to San Francisco in the early 1900s. Katrin's voice introduced each episode, "But first and foremost, I remember Mama."[13] Grief keepers remember various special things about their loved one.

Before my paternal grandfather died, he had a leg amputated, ending his ability to drive his tractor or truck — a devastating physical and emotional blow to a farmer. Over the last months of his life, suffering from phantom pain, he complained about the pain in the amputated limb. Emotional and spiritual phantom pain can also impact grievers. Alba Ambert's experience is intriguing: "Having lost my mother, I've gone through life with the pain of an amputated limb. The pain of a limb that has been sawn off, but that remains in the severed nerve, in the scar tissue. A phantom pain...After she died, I was adrift and a familiar unreality settled in me."[14]

In physical pain, the brain floods potent brain chemicals to dowse or dull the pain. In emotional pain, the brain releases memories. Unfortunately many individuals, believing that memories only make the pain more intense, refuse to show the memories hospitality. While writing this chapter, I hosted a dinner party for neighbors. Placing a bowl on the table, I remembered my mother had always served slaw in it. (I was not.) For a moment, I could hear her, "Dinner's ready. Go wash your face and hands." Even though I was busy, I stopped and showed hospitality to that snippet of memory.

Some people tolerate selected memories until, over time, those memories become threadbare. Aggressive remembering sends us digging through photo albums, letters, records, and boxes of stuff in basements, attics, closets, and storage sheds for tidbits of memories

207

that can trigger more complete memories. Aggressive remembering sends us on expeditions through the memories of others. Aggressive remembering turns some into sleuths looking for answers to questions — or secrets — about the deceased.

Deep in our memories are archives. Some stored memories wait for the right time to release into our consciousness. Months after my father's death, I learned that he had almost suffocated as a child. As he and his sister, aged four and five, played in the barn, a loft full of hay dislodged and buried them. Fortunately, their dog kept barking until my grandfather investigated and realized that Elma and Paul were under the hay. Digging frantically by hand, his yelling summoned my grandmother and farmhands who worked until my father and my aunt were extracted.

I had never heard the story before. For some reason, while writing a condolence letter to me, the memory resurfaced for my aunt and she passed it on to me.

〜 *The Reformation and remembering.* Historically, grievers have been encouraged to remember. Prayers for the souls of the departed were a specific way to remember them. The Reformation, however, by abolishing such prayers, drove some remembering functions underground. British sociologist Tony Walter has charged that "Protestantism is historically premised on banning intercourse between this world and the next."[15]

For centuries, a dominant theological influence was considered to be the communion of saints. Grief was kept through the spiritual exercises of praying for the dead, and honoring All Saints' Day. Christians commonly believed that only saints went directly into the presence of God; everyone else had to be purified through the fires of Purgatory. (And some individuals needed lots of prayers before they could be sprung!) Prayer cards with the name and date of death were distributed at Rosary services and funerals as a way of reminding individuals to pray for the soul of the dearly departed. Novelist Mary Higgins Clark recalled: "Mother had a stack of prayer cards for all her deceased friends and relatives. She was then seventy-six, and the list was long. It took her an hour to go through all of them each night before she went to bed. She liked to sit on a chair in the upstairs hall, where she claimed the light was better. It also was a good spot for her to overhear conversations taking place in the living room below."[16]

In medieval times, confraternities were organized to pray for the dead. For a fee paid in advance, individuals could arrange and guarantee prayers for their soul — in case a spouse remarried and, over time, abandoned the prayers or in case one died without children or estranged from one's children.

Over time, such excesses prompted Martin Luther and others to protest the belief in Purgatory. Soon the Protestants pointedly refused to pray for the dead — an action with significant implications on grief keeping. If salvation was solely by grace, the Reformers argued, how could prayers or remembrance by family, friends, or confraternities benefit the dead? Luther vigorously denounced vigils, requiems, funeral pomp, and Purgatory as worthless "popish abominations."

Later Luther reevaluated his polity: "The dead are still our brothers, and have not fallen from our community by death; we still remain members of a single body; therefore it is one of the duties of 'civic neighbourliness' to accompany the dead to the grave."[17] Luther advised followers: "When you have prayed once or twice, then let it be sufficient and commend them unto God,"[18] which is a polite way of saying: Get over it!

For a time, in some areas of seventeenth-century Germany, a corpse was carried to a grave and buried in absolute silence, without prayers, sermons, or singing; some Reformers even buried their dead at midnight.[19] Historian A. I. Dunlop labeled these as "sterile burials," and they complicated grief among the surviving family and friends, especially those who remained loyal to Rome. Had not the departed died trusting them to remember to pray for their souls? Some grievers resolved the conflict by secretly praying for their dead.

The Reformers threw out the baby, the bath, and the tub!

~ *Borrowing remembrance rituals.* Sometimes to remember meaningfully, we may borrow customs and venues from other traditions. Jewish mourners pray kaddish for eleven months for a parent, one month for others. Anne Brener comments, "Over the years, I have learned to use the kaddish as a way to communicate with the people I have lost. When I say the kaddish, I focus on the person I am remembering and think about what I would like to tell him or her."[20]

Leon Wieseltier disclosed that although he had not prayed in twenty years, after his father died, as a son "it was my duty" to pray kaddish three times a day. Even traveling, Wieseltier hunted for synagogues to join a *minyan,* the gathering of ten mourners who pray kaddish. "As I said kaddish for him, I remembered sometimes a friend who died in London two years ago and sometimes a friend who died in New York last year, and I prayed for them, too."[21] Wieseltier and others have discovered that what starts out as a duty evolves into a blessing.

When my mother died, I borrowed the tradition and prayed kaddish daily for eleven months, minus a day. (To pray longer than that time period implies the deceased was a great sinner.): "Glorified and sanctified be God's great name through the world, which He has created according to His will. May He establish His kingdom within your lifetime and the lifetime of the whole house of Israel, speedily and soon, and let us say, Amen. May His great name be praised unto all eternity. Exalted and praised, glorified and adored, extolled and revered be the name of the Holy One. Blessed is He beyond all song and psalm, beyond all praise mortal man can bestow upon him, and let us say, Amen. May life and abundant peace descend from heaven upon us and all Israel, and let us say, Amen. May the Creator of heavenly peace bestow peace upon us and all Israel, and let us say, Amen."[22]

As I wrote the first draft of this chapter, I pulled out my frayed copy of the kaddish and reread my notations from those early morning prayers. (I prayed kaddish once a day rather than the three times of traditional Jewish mourners.) Some days, certain words or phrases stayed with me. Over time, I modified phrases. "May the Creator of heavenly peace" became "May the Creator of the heavenly peace in which my mother sleeps." One December morning as I prayed that phrase, I recalled how much my mother had loved the carol "Silent Night," especially the concluding line, "Sleep in heavenly peace." That silent morning,

I heard the peace that became my peace. I shifted from mourner to grief keeper.

So great is kaddish tradition that some Jews call sons "my kaddish." They know, after death, they will be remembered when their sons say kaddish. In *Siddur Sim Shalom,* the book of worship used in Conservative Judaism, I found this supporting prayer: "In love we remember those who no longer walk this earth. We are grateful to God for these lives, for the joys we shared, and for the cherished memories that never fade. May God grant to those who mourn the strength to see beyond their sorrow, sustaining them despite their grief. May the faith that binds us to our loved ones be a continuing source of comfort."[23]

The kaddish prayer focuses on the greatness of God, the faithfulness of God, the longing for the kingdom of God. Hymns like "Now Thank We All Our God," "How Great Thou Art," or "Great Is Thy Faithfulness" serve as Christian versions of kaddish.

~ *The helpful Jewish traditions of* **yahrzeit** *and* **yizkor.** Jews also remember their dead through *yahrzeit* and *yizkor. Yahrzeit* is the observance of the anniversary of a death by reciting kaddish and attending a service at a synagogue or temple. Lighting a twenty-four-hour candle on the eve of *yahrzeit* is "not an occasion for renewed mourning," Simeon Maslin explained, but an initiation of a "day consecrated each year to the memory of the dead."[24] This prayer may lead the rememberer to a *mitzvot,* an act of charity, in honor of the deceased. In a sense, *yahrzeit* is a petition to God to remember the deceased even as the griever remembers them. One anniversary prayer begins, "May

God remember the soul of...who has gone to his [her] world."

Yizkor is a communal permission to keep the grief. I wish early Christians had adapted this observance as they borrowed other Jewish customs. The holy days — Yom Kippur, Shemini Atzeret, Pesach, and Shavout — provide occasions to acknowledge mourning communally. Although individuals generally pray *yizkor* in a synagogue or temple in the presence of other rememberers, some individuals pray in other meaningful places: "In this solemn hour, my thoughts turn to the memory of my dear and loving relatives who are no longer with me. Despite the passage of time and the absence of their physical form, I feel their presence, their love, and their influence. The power of their lives is still real, as real as when they were alive. They remain for me a tower of strength, a source of inspiration, and a constant influence for good. The values and lessons they transmitted to me and instilled within me still energize and motivate me. May they never lose their potency....I pray that these feelings of gratefulness never recede as I now recall those individuals who were closest and dearest to me. May their souls ever be linked with my soul, and may they rest in peace."[25]

Brener acknowledges that by asking God to remember the deceased, remembrance becomes a way to partner with God.[26] As a child I sang a peppy chorus, "Do, Lord, Oh do, Lord, Oh do remember me...way behind the blue." Now I sing, "Do, Lord, Oh do, Lord, Oh do remember them."

～ *Observing All Saints' Day.* Since the fourth century, Christians have observed a day for honoring "all the saints who from their labors rest," in the words of an anthem commonly sung on that day. Previously, saints were named during the celebration of the mass; however, because the list of saints grew long — which meant long masses — November 1 evolved as the day to honor dead saints liturgically.

Over time, some church fathers became concerned about those who had not been pious or saintly or those who had no one, particularly after a war, calamity, or plague, to pray for the repose of their souls. So All Souls' Day emerged as a day to remember liturgically all who had died.

The Reformers zealously sought to eradicate anything popish. Hence the celebration of these important liturgies was abandoned or in some places rooted out. In 1651, British Archbishop Grindal ordered that "no month-minds or yearly commemoration of the dead, nor any other superstitious ceremonies be observed or used which tend either to the maintenance of prayer for the dead or of popish purgatory."[27] Scattered historical evidence demonstrates that despite the efforts to reform funeral and grief rituals, remembrance traditions continued in much of England.

One custom that survived was the ringing of the village church bell both signaling a death and marking key anniversaries of a death. In many areas, the anniversary was called a minning day (abbreviated from reminding).

Today, the more fundamentalist the believer, the less likely that person is to have a ritual for remembering the dead other than Memorial Day, which is a civil holiday. There is growing interest in All Saints' Day beyond the traditional mainline Christians celebrators. This may be linked to the large number of boomers who have reached an age where one or both of their parents have died.

~ **Observing the Day of the Dead.** Hispanics have long observed liturgies and rituals for their dead, particularly Día de los Muertos, the Day of the Dead, an observance rooted in ancient Aztec culture. Early Catholic missionaries in South and Central America acknowledged the Little Feast of the Dead and the Great Feast of the Dead as significant and modified them. Rosalind Rosoff Beimler traces the origins of these recast rituals back to ancient Egypt.[28]

In this festive tradition, it is believed that the dead return to check up on their families around October 31. The Day of the Dead is a time to actively and aggressively remember, to visit the cemetery, gather families, and build altars called *ofredas* to honor the dead. According to Gina Hyams, "The ritual isn't about grief and solemnity; it is about remembering and feeling close to the dead,"[29] and, because of shared memories, feeling close to living family members. The Day of the Dead is a socially accepted time to revisit grief and work on unfinished issues with the dead.

The vigil begins at midnight on November 1 and goes through dawn on November 2, although celebrations vary in different localities. Extended families gather in homes or around family cemetery plots, bringing food, marigolds, and memories. Some families pray and serenade the dead while others toast their dead with shots of tequila or the deceased's favorite whiskey. While the dead are not seen, "their presence is felt,"[30] and their memories are cherished or sometimes amended.

Although the altar in the home does not have to be elaborate, much thought is given to what goes on the altar. Rememberers choose objects or artifacts "to embody the legacy of...loved ones and to entice their souls back to earth for a visit."[31] This grief work reminds families of their ties to one another. "Inviting children to participate in the process is a wonderful opportunity to pass on family stories, fostering a vital sense of connection with ancestral roots as well as assuaging the fear of death."[32] Some people find comfort in the knowledge that just as this altar is constructed for the dead, someday an altar will be constructed for them. Hyams offers guidance that is relevant to all grief keepers: "Think about your loved one's passions. What gave them pleasure? What made them tick? Remember good times you shared. Did they enjoy any hobbies? What sort of work did they do? Gather items that symbolize those memories — like a ticket stub from a concert you attended together, an autographed baseball, or a copy of a favorite novel. If they liked to sew, you could include a jar of buttons; if they gardened, a packet of seeds. Clothing and jewelry that the person wore are also powerful repositories of memory."[33]

Family members exchange memories as they plan and arrange their altar. Some use many candles because the flickering flames will provide light for the soul's passage home.

Day of the Dead activities and masses give grievers concrete ways to give voice to feelings of loyalty, affection, and longing for loved ones who have passed away.

Along with the growth of the Hispanic population in the United States, critics, particularly fundamentalist Christians, dismiss these shrines as ancestor worship; moralists decry the excesses of drinking and money ill spent. Enthusiasts respond that the Day of the Dead strengthens the enduring power of familial ties through memory. By honoring our loved ones' spirits in living color, a sense of continuity is maintained, even in a new country or community.

Given the growing move toward conservative Protestantism, some Hispanic evangelicals observe the day clandestinely for fear of religious censure. Conversely, family tensions erupt when those who have become Protestants do not observe the days and thereby seemingly disrespect the ancestors.

Some grievers create a personal Day of My Dead by creating a small display in their home (or on a website). Assemble photographs, candles, and marigolds — or a favorite flower of the deceased — and objects or items that symbolize the deceased, and create a centerpiece on a table. Spend time thinking about the loved one. Name that person's contributions to your life.

Go to a favorite restaurant of your loved one and order one of his or her favorite foods. Or at home prepare a favorite recipe or a dessert that the deceased loved.

Give yourself permission to remember creatively with all of your senses.

~ *Diversity and ancestor worship.* In the rich cultural diversity in America, some people practice ancestor worship. Although Christian missionaries have zealously attempted to root out the practice, immigrants have imported the tradition to this country. These practices honor the dead.

In a move-on-and-get-over-it culture, it is easy to discredit a ritual for honoring ancestors, particularly if we know little about the practice. Too many individuals know only their recent dead. Unless you are interested in genealogy, you probably know little of your family history beyond two generations removed. Many people have familial amnesia. Name your great-great-grandfathers; hint: you had eight. Most adults can name only one or two.

All it takes is a generation or two to forget an ancestor's name and stories, and collective familial memory becomes impoverished. At Tony Walter's father's funeral, a family friend used his Shona tradition to support the family in grief. Shonas believe that the spirits of the deceased can be kept alive by acknowledging the deceased as continuing members of the family and retaining them as participants in the survivor's biographies. After all, Walter observed, "We are who we are in part because of who he was, and we deny reality if we try to leave him entirely behind." In Western culture, saying that an individual is still alive suggests a sense of illusion that is transitional and, hopefully, will be discarded. Walters says for most Westerners the ultimate goal is living sans our deceased. "It is the other way around with the Shona. Straightforward and simple burial, not hiding the reality of death, means that they quickly accept that the person has died physically. [This] is a necessary preliminary to the long-term welcoming of the deceased back as one of the ancestors."

As a result, the dead person "is lost and re-found, rather than clung onto before being ultimately relinquished" or discarded.[34]

Kwanzaa is an African American end-of-the-year celebration, which begins on December 26 and has seven focuses for seven days. One day focuses on honoring ancestors.

~ *Observing Memorial Day.* The deaths of family and friends must be integrated into the emotional mix of our daily lives. Ask friends who still grieve the deaths of buddies in Normandy, Korea, Vietnam, or Iraq. As World War II veterans have aged, more are now willing to talk about their war experiences. Many came home determined to move on and to forget.

A long period of grieving in silence is ending, prompting the formation of ad hoc nostalgia brigades. During the dedication ceremonies for the Robert Dole Center at the University of Kansas, story tents were set up where veterans could take the stage and share their memories and losses. An editorial cartoon in the *Dallas Morning News* showed two GIs resting under a tree on a hill overlooking a military cemetery. One soldier asks, "Willie, y'think anyone'll remember us fifty years from now?" His friend answers, "Lord, Joe, I hope so."[35] Remembering is a healthy responsibility.

Memorial Day was once called Decoration Day. In an era before perpetual care — the cemetery fee for cutting the grass, trimming around the grave, and removing leaves and snow — tending the grave gave grievers a reason and unspoken permission to go to the cemetery. When the current World War II generation dies off, Memorial Day may be celebrated just as the first day of summer rather than as a day to remember our dead.

Amy Dickinson is a deliberate rememberer who has called for taking Memorial Day more seriously. Amy's extended family gathers that day in a park near her rural hometown to have a barbecue and play softball. "For us the best thing about the holiday is the part that has become an afterthought for many people — the remembering." The family gathers to remember relatives. It is also a time for cleaning, watering, and planting flowers and tending the graves. And remembering. "We read down the list of ancestors, going back to the Revolutionary War, whose names are etched on the granite memorial, and trade snippets of their lives. There is my great-uncle who in mid-life ran off with the circus. His sainted wife's stone sits forlorn, wedged into the grass. We also celebrate the ordinariness of our ancestors — the soldiers, teachers, farmers and parents who spent purposeful lives in this little town. Our visit to the cemetery is where we work out our connection to these people, and to one another."[36]

Dickinson urges: "Before you stoke up the grill this year, raise a glass to the people who came before you — those who fought for our country or who tended the home fires," and help your family remember.[37]

Memorial Day also offers an occasion to forgive and reconcile. Columbus, Mississippi, claims that the celebration of Memorial Day began there in 1866. As the legend goes, several ladies were decorating Confederate graves and came upon the graves of several dozen Yankees. In an act of grace, they also decorated those graves. Many acts of grace, as well as decoration, take place in cemeteries on Memorial Days.

William Gladstone, four times the prime minister of England, observed, "Show me the manner in which a nation or a community cares for its dead. I will measure exactly the sympathies of its people, their respect for the laws of the land, and their loyalty to high ideas."[38] Were Mr. Gladstone alive today, he might easily conclude that Memorial Day is about big sales at shopping malls and department stores, ball games and fireworks, barbecues and picnics, and trips to the beach.

Memorial Day is more than placing flowers or a small American flag on a grave. It is about stopping to remember our dead.

In 2000, Mike Thompson drew a cartoon that depicted a car speeding by a cemetery that had an American flag at half-mast for Memorial Day. The driver is reciting the packing list: "Picnic basket, cooler, charcoal grill, hot dogs, lemonade, Frisbee..." Then, "Did we forget anything?"

Historian Robert Dallek concluded that Jackie Kennedy's "effort to lionize Kennedy must have produced a therapeutic shield against immobilizing grief" that she initially felt. Just days after the assassination she invited historian William Manchester to Hyannisport to discuss a family-supported biography. Jackie "understood that no one was going to forget him; rather, her concern was how the world would remember him."[39]

Not all of us can rely on a noted historian to preserve our family's memories. While delivering lectures at Spring Arbor University, driving between the campus and my motel, I kept noticing a large sign, "Bill Carpenter will never be forgotten." Finally I asked someone, "Who was Bill Carpenter?"

Bill, a runner, was struck and killed along the shoulder of Spring Arbor Road by a driver who did not see him. Friends and family erected and maintain the sign.

"It's always nice to be remembered," says an aged friend of mine.

On the long journey to a far place, give yourself permission to remember.

You Have Permission
to Keep Your Grief

I found that with time I actually feel my mother's presence in my life more than ever. As I go through different stages in my own life, I talk with my mother and know that she is with me. I really think that I am closer than ever before.   —Sally Higgins[1]

On a visit to London, while I was browsing a newspaper, a phrase at the end of an obituary — "No mourning" — surprised me.[2] No mourning. What did that mean? Surely it could not mean no mourning! Some type of British code, perhaps. When I called *The Times* seeking clarification, an editor's tone implied that I must be dense.

"No mourning. You know, no going on and on about it . . . crying and all that." That British phrase captures the attitude of many on this side of the Atlantic: there should be little or no mourning. I expect soon to find the phrase in obituaries in American newspapers.

~ **Grief keepers are patient.** Grief keepers must function in a society where impatience is an art form. Americans are not good at keeping grief but rather are impatient to have it done with, not unlike a root canal or income taxes. Many want grief to be, at best, an inconvenience to be navigated in our fix-it culture. Grievers repeatedly hear, "You should be over it by now." We nudge grievers or scold them, depending on our assessment of their ability to move along.

Perhaps you remember that moment in *Our Town* when the cast sings, "Blessed be the tie that binds." Unfortunately, this culture values severing bonds. Nothing is permanent. Kathrin Boerner and Jutta Heckhausen conclude that a "breaking bonds orientation" is the inevitable byproduct of a modernist worldview, which prizes efficiency and rationality. Anything, even death, that challenges those virtues must be quickly recovered from and must not be allowed to influence one's life, profession, or goals.[3]

Newspaper stories can have a significant impact. Many readers caught the story of Bill Cosby returning to work after his son's death: "Bill Cosby has decided to return to work next week, resuming the taping of his sitcom, *Cosby,* while the Los Angeles police continue to investigate the slaying of his son, Ennis, last week. Several people connected with the CBS show said Cosby made the decision out of concern for those who work on it and out of a sense that his son would want him to do so."[4]

No one wanted to see Bill Cosby incapacitated with grief. "Way to go, Bill!" many concluded. Victoria Alexander, a suicide survivor, commented on the reluctance to grieve: "Our society has little tolerance for grief. We expect it to be discreet, tidy, and above all, short-lived. Memorial services, burials, wakes ... are appointed occasions for expressing loss and grief. Once these rituals have been completed, the survivors are supposed to grieve privately and be done."[5]

In the debate over a public memorial for the 114 persons who died when two Hyatt hotel walkways collapsed, in a letter to the editor Dan Mercer demanded, "Why not grieve within your own heart, privately, and with dignity?"[6] It matters when it was your son, father, aunt, or cousin who died in that place.

~ *Grief keepers recognize grief as a place between what was and what is yet to be.* Grief keepers do not get over it, move on, get closure, heal, or recover from significant losses. Rather, over time, grief keepers weave their loss into the mosaic of their life narratives. For some people grief is an opportunity to reassess their life views. By engaging their grief, grievers gain a clearer sense of what is important, precious, and valuable in a disposable, throwaway society.

Matthew Shepard's horrific death in Wyoming in 1998 shocked the nation. Matthew's mother, Judy, found herself grieving in the media spotlight. Many have found comfort in her summation of her apprenticeship with grief: "The past year has been a learning experience for the entire family. One thing brought painfully to all our minds and hearts is that we take far too much for granted. We think that there will be a tomorrow to talk, hug, discuss, settle questions, declare our love, share our ideas, and be at peace. We have found that this is not the case. We should never wait until later to share our feelings. Life is too short. At the same time, we realize the waste of energy in regrets. One can get lost in regret and forget about the wonderful, happy memories that are part of everyone's life. Grief is a very individual and personal experience. Everyone goes through it their own way. Without the love and support of our family and friends, this year would have been even more difficult."[7] Grief keepers do not rush past their days of grief to what is yet to be.

～ *Grief keepers are open to grief's lessons.* Rather than attempting to manage their grief, grievers befriend the grief. While grievers get bitter, grief keepers get wiser.

Judy Shepard gained wisdom as a grief keeper, and in sharing her insights she passed along some of that wisdom.

We cannot continue to keep grief privately, in the isolation of our residence or the sanctuary of our own mind and heart, out of public view. Every griever knows something that another griever needs to know. Grief never touches us without leaving a seed of wisdom.

Americans have appropriated Queen Elizabeth's rule for the royal family — particularly for her grandsons following Diana's death: "Never show emotion in public." William and Harry were expected "to set their faces and carry on, no matter what their private feelings might be."[8]

Maybe princes in castles must live that way, but most individuals have the choice to grieve with others.

～ *Grief keepers model grief keeping skills.* Early in the AIDS epidemic, one university professor could not acknowledge the death of her brother. To inquirers she passed off her tears and red eyes as an allergy. The story went unchallenged until one day when a colleague walked into her office, shut the door, and said, "It's not allergies. What is going on?" As she released the story of her brother's death, her colleague began to cry.

"My brother died with AIDS, too," her colleague said softly. All that time that the woman had been hiding her grief, just doors away a colleague was grieving a similar loss. Telling narratives, the stories of our loved ones and their death, frees us from the bonds of isolated grief. Ironically, in an institution devoted to knowledge, they both had hidden their grief. In Jesus's words, they had hidden their light under a bushel. In a setting that understood grief intellectually rather than emotionally, they began to model grief keeping. They started saying their brothers' names. They dared to tell the truth about the causes of the two deaths. Through disclosure, both found courage to model grief without apology to a large university community.[9]

In 2002, the *New York Times* devoted two-thirds of a page to chronicle the lingering grief of Morton and Esther-Ann Asch, whose daughter, Jennifer, had died of an acute asthma attack in 1976 — a quarter century earlier. The article was titled "An Unending Journey through Faith and Heartbreak: Long after a 9-Year-Old Girl's Death, Her Family Continues to Question the Hand of God." A large photo captured the sad Asches, sitting on their bed, Jennifer's picture in the foreground; the caption read, "Morton and Esther-Ann Asch still grieve."[10] Over coffee and bagels, many readers undoubtedly grumbled, "They need to get a life!"

But grief keeping is a part of life.

~ **Grief keepers take care of their hearts.** In the experience-forged words of Dawn Siegrist Waltman, whose daughter was born dead, grief is life with a hole in the heart, "a hole that some day feels so huge it could actually engulf me." Physicians have counseled parents of babies born with a small hole in their heart not to worry; the child will outgrow it. Waltman believes that grievers need time, too. Not time to get over their loss, but time to realize that the myriad ways grievers try to overcome a grief will not fill that hole. Waltman believed that as time passed: "My heart will grow as well. As I love and am loved, my heart will grow even more. And as my heart steadily grows, the hole will seem smaller and to some degree less painful. But the hole and the ache that accompanies it will never go away. And I do not want it to."[11] Through grief, Dawn has become wise.

~ **Grief keepers commemorate their loss.** Eleanor Elkins Widener endowed the library at Harvard University to honor her son, Harry, class of 1907, a rare book dealer who drowned on the *Titanic*. Harry had planned to donate his personal book collection to Harvard once the university built a new library. Harry's dream was fulfilled and exceeded by his mother's generous memorial gift. Widener Library, completed in 1915, has more than sixty-five miles of bookshelves with almost three million volumes.[12] Thousands of Harvard students, professors, alumni, and visiting scholars, have used the library without knowing the story behind the gift.

I remembered the story of Widener Library when I walked through the magnificent new Waggoner Library at my alma mater, Trevecca Nazarene University. However, I noticed an absence of art. Months later at an estate sale, I found two life-sized bronze sculptures that I bought and donated to the library. One, a young boy drinking a beverage, sits in the foyer because beverages are not allowed in the library! The other, a girl reading a book, sits inside. A small plaque reads, "These sculptures were given in memory of Mary Catherine Eckert Smith and all the other mothers who sacrificed so their daughters and sons could have Trevecca educations."

Although my mother only completed the eighth grade, she had a dream that her youngest son would have "an education." Struggling with dementia, she attended my doctoral graduation. Although I am not sure how much she understood, as my family left that night, she whispered, "Honey, I am so proud of you." For decades in the future, my mother's sacrifices will be honored in that space. I doubt that I would have made that gift had I not known the story of Eleanor Widener keeping the grief for Harry.

Grief keepers borrow from other traditions to facilitate keeping their grief. Rob Hosick was killed before his fifteenth birthday. His father, David, a Presbyterian minister, recalled, "In an instant of learning of Rob's death, however, my reliance on the sovereign control of God was undone. The portrait of the sovereign God faded from my view." That was a significant problem for someone who served as one of God's field reps. So what did he do? "After Rob's funeral, I purchased a crucifix and placed it on the wall above Rob's empty chair at our dinner table. Displaying a crucifix is a no-no for us Reformed types, but every evening, when I had to stare at Rob's empty chair in front of me, I could lift my eyes to the crucifix and remember God had suffered a grief such as mine."[13]

Small acts support grief keeping. My friend Diane called a golden oldies radio station and requested her brother Martin's favorite song be played on his birthday. The request reminded listeners that they too could request a deceased loved one's favorite song.

My friend Dennis ran the Chicago Marathon wearing a T-shirt with his son's name on the front and the years of his life on the back. Before the race began, another runner walked over and asked, nodding to the name,

"Was that your son?" In those moments, two grief keeping fathers discovered a bond stronger than running marathons.

One afternoon as I walked the panels of the AIDS Quilt, I heard a woman sobbing, "I can't find my son's name." Immediately, another mother slipped up and whispered, "I will help you." I lingered at a particular panel to listen to their conversation about their sons and then walked on. An hour later, the grief keepers were still at the same spot.

A memorial act may be buying a brick in a courtyard, which will be a witness to a life lived and remembered. That brick also may be an invitation to someone to buy a brick for their loved one.

~ *Grief keepers anticipate the redemption of the promise.* Jesus offered no time line for the fulfillment of his promise that mourners will be comforted. Millions of visitors have toured the Precious Memories Center near Carthage, Missouri, where Sam Butcher has painted murals on the chapel ceiling. In one mural, at the entrance to heaven, a small sign is posted, "No crying allowed."

In the book of Revelation, John described a loud voice proclaiming, "He will wipe every tear from their eyes. There will be no more death or mourning or crying or pain."[14] Why does God not say, "Hey, knock off the crying! This is heaven!" Why does God wipe away tears? Do you remember the difference between a parent saying, "Stop your crying!" and a parent holding you and wiping away your tears?

There will be a line for grievers until each finally stands in front of God. The same hand that, in James Weldon Johnson's classic description, "scooped up the clay" and made humankind will wipe away every tear. In that moment, Jesus's promise, "They shall be comforted," will be redeemed. And at that moment, some will lay down their faithfully kept griefs. Joy will erupt like Fourth of July fireworks!

Above all the joy you will hear the laughter of Jesus, who knew this day would come.

All who kept their grief will, at last, be comforted.

Reunion has long been a nourishing hope for grief keepers. It has kept some sane. It has given some the courage to get out of bed and face the demands of the day.

~ **Let us keep our grief.** In the Eucharist after the bread is broken, the celebrant says, "Christ our Passover is sacrificed for us," and the people respond, "Therefore let us keep the feast."[15] I wish funeral celebrants would lead us to say, "Therefore let us keep the grief." The invitation would be plural, "let *us* keep the feast." We all need help keeping our griefs.

Children can help us keep a grief. Elliott loved his grandmother, and, on her birthday after her death, he was perplexed because they couldn't have birthday cake and ice cream at dinner.

"Oh, Elliott," his mother replied, "we can still have cake and celebrate Grandma's birthday."

"But how will she get her piece of cake?" Then he answered, "I know. We could send it up to heaven on a spaceship." His mother explained that the cake would get stale. Elliott pondered that. That night, at dinner, as they gathered around the cake, Elliott said, "We have to sing 'Happy Birthday' so loud that Grandma can hear it all the way up in heaven!"

The Kellers sang "Happy Birthday" louder than it had ever been sung in that household. I have a hunch that God called Grandma Dot over and said, "Check this out. That's quite a grandson you have."

In Genesis we get no psychological insights into Abraham's grief for Sarah other than the brief observation, "Abraham went to mourn for Sarah and to weep over her. Then Abraham rose from beside his dead wife."[16] That's not much insight into the grief of a man married to a woman for almost a century. I find Abraham's action more intriguing in the Revised Standard Version, "Then Abraham rose up."

The narrative does not report that Abraham, revered in three world religions, got over Sarah or moved on. Only that he "rose up."

Someone asked a child, "And how old are you?"

"Four," she answered.

"And when will you be five?" the questioner asked, expecting to learn the birthday of the child.

"When I'm finished being four."

Not surprisingly, most people want to know when they will be over their grief. I answer them, borrowing sentiments from the child, "Not until you have thoroughly kept the grief."

We have doorkeepers, lighthouse-keepers, peace-keepers, beekeepers, timekeepers, and zookeepers. What this culture desperately needs is grief keepers.

As pilgrims on a long journey to a far place, be proud to be a grief keeper.

Sources Cited

The Right to Keep Your Grief (pages 9–17)

1. Barbara K. Roberts, *Death without Denial, Grief without Apology: A Guide for Facing Death and Loss* (Troutdale, Ore.: NewSage Press, 2002), 7.
2. Hendrik Booraem, *Young Hickory: The Making of Andrew Jackson* (Dallas: Taylor Trade Publishing, 2001), 110–11.
3. Andrew Burstein, *The Passions of Andrew Jackson* (New York: Knopf, 2003), 172.
4. Ibid., 173.
5. Barbara Lazear Ascher, *Landscape without Gravity: A Memoir of Grief* (Harrison, N.Y.: Delphinum Books, 1992), 98.
6. Victoria Alexander, *Words I Never Thought to Speak: Stories of Life in the Wake of Suicide* (New York: Lexington Books, 1991), x.
7. George H. W. Bush, *All the Best: My Life in Letters and Other Writings* (New York: Scribner, 1999), 578.
8. David Goldstein, "Carnahan Thanks Colleagues for Support in Farewell Address," *Kansas City Star,* November 19, 2002, A4.
9. Richard Pyle and Horst Fass, *Lost over Laos: A True Story of Tragedy, Mystery, and Friendship* (New York: De Capo Press, 2003), 231.
10. Matthew 5:4.

You Have Permission to Grieve as Long as You Need (pages 18–38)

1. Barbara K. Roberts, *Death without Denial, Grief without Apology: A Guide for Facing Death and Loss* (Troutdale, Ore.: NewSage Press, 2002), 7.
2. Helen O'Neil, "Mass. Attorney Uncovers Truth about Navy Ship," *Lakeland [Florida] Ledger,* January 26, 2003, A16.
3. Jules Crittenden, "1945 U-boat Attack Survivors to Gather in Quincy," *Boston Herald,* June 3, 2002, 3.
4. Ibid.
5. Ecclesiasticus 38:20–21.
6. G. Weatherhead, "The Mourning After: 10 Steps to Be Healed from the Wound of Grief," *Preacher's Magazine* (September, October, November 2002): 43.
7. Hope Edelman, *Motherless Daughters: The Legacy of Loss* (New York: Addison-Wesley, 1994), 5.
8. Albert F. Bayly, "Lord, Whose Love through Humble Service," in *Amazing Grace: Hymn Texts for Devotional Use,* ed. Bert Polman, Marilyn Kay Stulken, and James Rawlings Sydnor (Louisville, Ky.: Westminster John Knox Press, 1961, 1994), 249–50.
9. Brian A. Wren, "Telling Truth through Tearful Songs," *Journal for Preachers* 26, no. 2 (Lent 2003): 22.
10. Ecclesiastes 3:1, 4.
11. Thomas Lynch, "What Makes a Good Funeral Director: An Interview with Poet-Undertaker Thomas Lynch," *The Director* (December 2002): 35.

12. Dennis C. McGee, "The Sum of All the Parts," *The Director* (November 2002): 80.

13. Ibid.

14. Ellen Goodman, "Mourning Gets the Bum's Rush," *Kansas City Star,* August 2, 1998, B7.

15. Carl Sferrazza Anthony, *Florence Harding: The First Lady, the Jazz Age, and the Death of America's Most Scandalous President* (New York: Quill, 1998), 473.

16. Ibid., 482.

17. George W. Bush, "Bush's Speech," *Kansas City Star,* September 15, 2001, A12.

18. Harold Ivan Smith, "As I See It: To Resolve Grief, Give It a Voice," *Kansas City Star,* September 11, 2002, B6.

19. Keith S. Sollenberger, "Don't Overdo WTC Memorials," letter to the editor, *USA Today,* June 3, 2002, 11A.

20. John 11:35.

21. John 11:38.

22. Goodman, "Mourning Gets the Bum's Rush," B7.

23. Ibid.

24. Margaret Truman, *Bess W. Truman* (New York: Macmillan, 1986), 30.

25. David Goldstein and Brian Burnes, "Truman Diary from '47 Found," *Kansas City Star,* July 11, 2003, A6.

26. Bush, *All the Best,* 443.

27. Ibid., 451.

28. Tim Dahlberg, "Nicklaus Respects Mom's Dying Wish," *Dallas Morning News,* August 17, 2000, B1.

29. "Death Overshadows Schumacher's Win," *Kansas City Star,* April 21, 2003, C7.

30. Marc Shapiro, *Pure Goldie: The Life and Career of Goldie Hawn* (New York: Birch Lane Press/Carol Publishing Group, 1998), 166–67.

31. Anna Quindlen, "Death Carves a Chasm of Loss Deep in the Center of Life," *Kansas City Star,* May 5, 1994, C5.

32. *Dorland's Illustrated Medical Dictionary,* 28th ed. (Philadelphia: W. B. Saunders, 1994), 1059.

33. J. William Worden, *Grief Counseling and Grief Therapy: A Handbook for the Mental Health Practitioner,* 2nd ed. (New York: Springer, 1991), 18.

34. Lesley Brown, ed., *The New Shorter Oxford English Dictionary on Historical Principles,* vol. 1: A–M (Oxford, U.K.: Clarendon Press, 1993), 531.

35. "States Debate Roadside Shrine Ban," *Kansas City Star,* July 13, 2003, A6.

36. Bob Herbert, "Racism and the G.O.P.," *New York Times,* December 12, 2002, A35.

37. In James A. Fussell, "For Sister, a Long and Painful Wait, Then Heartache," *Kansas City Star,* February 3, 2003, A1, A6.

38. Harold Ivan Smith, *Kansas City Star,* February 14, 2003, A6.

39. Brett McNeil and Joshua S. Howes, "Perfect Night for a Party Ends in Agony," *Chicago Tribune,* July 1, 2003, sec. 1, pp. l, 15.

40. Tony Rizzo, "Kemp Father Cautious about Tip Involving Rape Suspect," *Kansas City Star,* February 11, 2003, A1.

41. Del Jones, "Burger King CEO Hopes to Help by Sharing His Grief," *USA Today,* November 14, 2001, 2B.

42. Sherwin B. Nuland, *How We Die: Reflections on Life's Final Chapter* (New York: Knopf, 1994), xviii.

43. Sherwin B. Nuland, *Lost in America: My Life with My Father* (New York: Alfred N. Knopf, 2003), no pagination.

44. Ibid.

45. Genesis 32:26.

46. John Claypool, *Tracks of a Fellow Struggler: How to Handle Grief* (Waco, Tex.: Word, 1974), 14.

47. John Claypool, *Mending the Heart* (Boston: Cowley Press, 1999), xiv.

48. Ibid., 63.

49. Worden, *Grief Counseling and Grief Therapy,* 18.

50. Claypool, *Tracks of a Fellow Struggler,* 102.

51. [Abigail Van Buren], "Dear Abby: Poem Moves Many," *Kansas City Star,* June 21, 1996, E2.

You Must Make Room to Keep Your Grief (pages 39–59)

1. Henry Taylor, *Philip Van Artevelde,* Part i, Act i.

2. Edmund Morris, *The Rise of T. R.* (New York: Coward, McGann and Geoghegan, 1979), 244.

3. Jan Jarboe Russell, *Lady Bird: A Biography of Mrs. Johnson* (New York: Scribner, 1999), 53.

4. Ibid., 54–55.

5. Ibid., 55.

6. Cynthia Anderson, *The Winchester Mystery House* (San Jose, Calif.: Winchester Mystery House, 1997), 11, 41.

7. L. E. Zimmerman, "Newcomb, Louise Le Monnier," in *Notable American Women, 1607–1950: A Biographical Dictionary,* ed. Edward T. James (Cambridge, Mass.: Belknap Press of Harvard University Press, 1971), 2:619.

8. H. W. Brands, *Theodore Roosevelt: The Last Romantic* (New York: Basic Books, 1997), 194.

9. Condoleezza Rice, "Acknowledge That You Have an Obligation to Search for the Truth," address to the Graduating Class of Stanford University, June 16, 2002.

10. Susan Eisenhower, *Mrs. Ike: Memories and Reflections on the Life of Mamie Eisenhower* (New York: Farrar, Straus & Giroux, 1996), 69.

11. Ibid., 74.

12. Stephen Ambrose, *Eisenhower: Soldier and President* (New York: Simon & Schuster, 1990), 38.

13. Susan Eisenhower, *Mrs. Ike,* 66–72.

14. James MacGregory Burns and Susan Dunn, *The Three Roosevelts: Patrician Leaders Who Transformed America* (New York: Atlantic Monthly Press, 2001), 33.

15. Gerhard Brendler, *Martin Luther: Theology and Revolution,* trans. Claude R. Foster Jr. (New York: Oxford University Press, 1991), 344.

16. Jack McLaughlin, *Jefferson and Monticello: The Biography of a Builder* (New York: Henry Holt, 1988), 201.

17. George Hagman, "Beyond Decathexis: Toward a New Psychoanalytic Understanding and Treatment of Mourning," in *Meaning Reconstruction and the Experience of Loss,* ed. Robert A. Neimeyer (Washington, D.C.: American Psychological Association, 2001), 25.

18. Cited in Victor Parachin, "When Is Mourning Finished?" *The Director* (April 2002): 12.

19. Kenneth Ackerman, *Dark Horse: The Surprise Election and Political Murder of James A. Garfield* (New York: Avalon, 2003), 438.

20. Skip Wood, "Solemn, Eerie Return: Dale, Jr. Crashes, Rain Stalls 400 in 1st Race after Earnhardt Death," *USA Today*, February 26, 2001, C1.

21. Ibid.

22. Ibid., C2.

23. 1 Thessalonians 4:13.

24. N. T. Wright, *The Resurrection of the Son of God*, vol. 3 of *Christian Origins and the Question of God* (Minneapolis: Fortress, 2003), 217.

25. F. van der Meer, *Augustine the Bishop: The Life and Work of a Father of the Church*, trans. Brian Battershaw and G. R. Lamb (New York: Sheed & Ward, 1961), 495.

26. Theodore G. Tappert, Willem J. Kooiman, and Lowell C. Green, *The Mature Luther*, vol. 3: *Martin Luther Lectures* (Decorah, Iowa: Luther College Press, 1959), 68.

27. Ackerman, *Dark Horse*, 426–27.

28. Peter Hay, *All the Presidents' Ladies: Anecdotes of the Women behind the Men in the White House* (New York: Viking, 1988), 283.

29. Diane Beresh, "Sirach," in *The New Interpreter's Study Bible* (Nashville: Abingdon, 2003), 1499.

30. Robert Sobel, *Coolidge: An American Enigma* (Washington, D.C.: Regnery, 1998), 297.

31. Cited in Rick Hampson, "75 Years Later, History More Kind to Coolidge," *USA Today*, July 31, 1998, 10A.

32. William Manchester, *American Caesar: Douglas MacArthur* (Boston: Little, Brown, 1978), 164.

33. D. Clayton James, *The Years of MacArthur*. Volume 1: 1880–1941 (Boston: Houghton Mifflin, 1970), 495.

You Have Permission to Ignore the Stages of Grief (pages 60–84)

1. Barbara K. Roberts, *Death without Denial, Grief without Apology: A Guide for Facing Death and Loss* (Troutdale, Ore.: NewSage Press, 2002), 78–79.

2. Donna McGuire, "Hyatt Impossible to Forget," *Kansas City Star*, www.kcstar.com/projects/hyatt/main.html, July 15, 2001.

3. Robert A. Neimeyer, *Lessons of Loss: A Guide to Coping* (New York: McGraw-Hill/Primis Custom Publishing, 1998), 84–85.

4. Ibid., 88.

5. Edmund Hansen, "All My Heart Leaked through My Pen," *The Lutheran* (March 2002): 23.

6. Neimeyer, *Lessons of Loss*, 88.

7. Mary Sanchez, "KC Parents of Soldier Killed in Barracks to Meet with General," *Kansas City Star*, March 13, 2003, B3.

8. Neimeyer, *Lessons of Loss*, 89.

9. Ibid.

10. Richard Hough, *Victoria and Albert* (New York: St. Martin's Press, 1996), 208.

11. Elizabeth Longford, ed., *The Oxford Book of Royal Anecdotes* (New York: Oxford University Press, 1989), 406.

12. See Joe Morella and Edward Z. Epstein, *Paul and Joanne: A Biography of Paul Newman and Joanne Woodward* (New York: Delacorte, 1988).

13. Grace Hobson, "Philippine Ordeal a Riveting Testimony," *Kansas City Star*, June 15, 2003, H7.

14. Mubarak Dahir, "September 11: Are All Survivors Equal?" *The Advocate* (September 17, 2002): 26.

15. Roberts, *Death without Denial*, 78–79.

16. Michael Bloch, *The Duchess of Windsor* (New York: St. Martin's Press, 1996), 217.

17. Thomas Attig, *The Heart of Grief: Death and the Search for Lasting Love* (New York: Oxford University Press, 2000), 61.

18. Ibid.

19. J. William Worden, *Grief Counseling and Grief Therapy: A Handbook for the Mental Health Practitioner*, 2nd ed. (New York: Springer, 1991), 47.

20. C. S. Lewis, *A Grief Observed* (New York: Bantam, 1961), 63.

21. Christopher Andersen, *The Day Diana Died* (New York: William Morrow, 1998), 233.

22. Thomas Lynch, "Good Grief: An Undertaker's Reflections," *Christian Century* (July 26, 2003): 21.

23. Ralph David Abernathy, *And the Walls Came Tumbling Down* (New York: Harper & Row, 1989), 444.

24. Ibid., 448.

25. Ibid.

26. Cited in John A. Peterson, "Dream of Burial at Arlington to Come 35 Years Late," *Kansas City Star,* May 29, 2003, A4.

27. M. J. Ryan, *The Power of Patience: How to Slow the Rush and Enjoy More Happiness, Success, and Peace Every Day* (New York: Conari Press, 2003), 3.

28. Morella and Epstein, *Paul and Joanne,* 284.

29. Ibid., 285.

30. Robert Sobel, *Coolidge: An American Enigma* (Washington, D.C.: Regnery, 1998), 296.

31. Worden, *Grief Counseling and Grief Therapy,*, 16.

32. V. D. Volkan, "Complicated Mourning," *Annual of Chicago Institute of Psychoanalysis* 12 (1985): 326.

33. See Helen Bryan, *Martha Washington: First Lady of Liberty* (New York: John Wiley, 2002).

34. Carl Sferrazza Anthony, *Florence Harding: The First Lady, the Jazz Age, and the Death of America's Most Scandalous President* (New York: Quill, 1998), 486.

35. Ibid.

36. Ibid., 489.

37. Ibid.

38. Ibid.

39. Charisse Jones, "Sorority of the Young: New Mothers Cope after Iraq War," *USA Today,* May 29, 2004, A1.

40. Ibid., A2.

41. Cited in ibid.

42. Cited in ibid.

43. Tony Walter, "A New Model of Grief: Bereavement and Biography," *Mortality* 1, no. 1 (1996): 12.

44. S. R. Shuchter and Sidney Zistook, "The Dexamethasone Suppression Test in Acute Grief," *American Journal of Psychiatry* 243 (1986): 879–81.

45. Walter, "A New Model of Grief," 11.

46. Alexandria K. Mosca, *Grave Undertakings: Mortician by Day, Model by Night: One Woman's True-Life Adventures* (Far Hills, N.J.: New Horizon Press, 2003), 287.

47. C. A. Corr, "Coping with Dying: Lessons That We Should and Should Not Learn from the Work of Elisabeth Kübler-Ross," *Death Studies* 17 (1993): 73–74.

You Have Permission to Lament (pages 85–105)

1. Barbara Lazear Ascher, *Landscape without Gravity: A Memoir of Grief* (Harrison, N.Y.: Delphinum Books, 1992), 98.
2. Frederic Guelton, "Foch," *Le Magazine de la Guerre* 8 (June–July 2002): 45.
3. Martin Gilbert, *The First World War: A Complete History* (New York: Henry Holt, 1994), 56.
4. Lottie Healy Jackson, Letter to Harry S. Truman, Truman Presidential Library, August 6, 1947.
5. F. J. Bowman, Letter to Harry S. Truman, Truman Presidential Library, August 31, 1947.
6. Philip Hersh, "Nike Takes a Stand on New Olympic Medals," *Chicago Tribune,* July 3, 2003, sec. 4, p. 3.
7. Sue Monk Kidd, *The Secret Life of Bees* (New York: Viking, 2002), 23.
8. Ann Weems, *Psalms of Lament* (Louisville, Ky.: Westminster John Knox Press, 1995), 98.
9. Judith Manners, "Widows Don't Need More Bad Advice," *Kansas City Star,* July 16, 2003, F10.
10. Truman Presidential Library, August 6, 1947.
11. Cited in Jennifer Fleischner, *Mrs. Lincoln and Mrs. Keckly: The Remarkable Story of the Friendship between a First Lady and a Former Slave* (New York: Broadway Books, 2003), 142.
12. Ronald Barrett, "Affirming and Reclaiming African-American Funeral Rites," *The Director* (October 1994): 36–40.
13. 1 Samuel 1:26.
14. www.progressiveaustin.org/mlkulogy/htm.
15. Dan Barry and Steven Greenhouse, "John William Perry: A Full Time, and Then Some," *New York Times,* October 30, 2001, B11.
16. Walter Mondale, cited in *Respectfully Quoted: A Dictionary of Quotations Requested from the Congressional Research Service,* ed. S. Platt (Washington, D.C.: Library of Congress, 1989), 233.
17. Christopher Andersen, *The Day John Died* (New York: William Morrow, 2000), 63.
18. Julia Cameron, *Prayers for a Nonbeliever: A Story of Faith* (New York: Jeremy P. Tarcher/Putnam, 2003), 44.
19. Robert A. Neimeyer, *Lessons of Loss: A Guide to Coping* (New York: McGraw-Hill/Primis Custom Publishing, 1998), 94.
20. Barbara K. Roberts, *Death without Denial, Grief without Apology: A Guide for Facing Death and Loss* (Troutdale, Ore.: NewSage Press, 2002), 57.
21. James Robert Parish, *Rosie: Rosie O'Donnell's Biography* (New York: Carroll & Graft, 1997), 5.
22. Dietrich Bonhoeffer, *Life Together,* trans. John W. Doberstein (New York: Harper & Row, 1954), 99.
23. Martin Kasindorf, "Some 9/11 Families Choose Lawsuits over Federal Fund," *USA Today,* July 14, 2003, A1.
24. See Harold Ivan Smith, "The Day the President's Baby Died," *The Director* (July 2003): 24–26.
25. Dwight Eisenhower, *At Ease: Stories I Tell My Friends* (Garden City, N.Y.: Doubleday, 1967), 304–5.

You Have Permission to Be Angry at God
(pages 106–126)

1. Rebecca Jones, *The President Has Been Shot! True Stories of the Attacks on Ten Presidents* (New York: Puffin, 1995), 47.

2. Ibid., 48.

3. Ibid., 53.

4. Donna Schaper, *Mature Grief: When a Parent Dies* (Boston: Cowley Press, 2003), 53–54.

5. C. S. Lewis, *A Grief Observed* (New York: Bantam, 1961), 25.

6. Ibid., xiv.

7. *The Book of Common Prayer and Administration of the Sacraments and Other Rites and Ceremonies of the Church* (New York: Seabury Press, 1979), 355.

8. Genesis 2:25.

9. Louis B. Smedes, "What's God Up To? A Father Grieves the Loss of a Child," *Christian Century* (May 3, 2003): 38.

10. Ibid.

11. Ibid.

12. Lewis, *A Grief Observed,* 5.

13. C. Everett Koop and Elizabeth Koop, *Sometimes Mountains Move* (Wheaton, Ill.: Tyndale House, 1979), 93.

14. Jennifer Fleischner, *Mrs. Lincoln and Mrs. Keckly: The Remarkable Story of the Friendship between a First Lady and a Former Slave* (New York: Broadway Books, 2003), 231.

15. Ibid., 230.

16. Cited in David Van Biema, "When God Hides His Face, *Time* (July 16, 2001): 62–64.

17. Job 38:1–2.

18. Job 1:1.

19. Job 1:20–21.

20. Lewis, *A Grief Observed,* 76.

21. Schaper, *Mature Grief,* 58.

22. Matthew 27:46.

23. William Sloane Coffin, "Alex's Death," in *The Book of Eulogies,* ed. Phyllis Theroux (New York: Scribner, 1997), 345.

24. Ibid.

25. Rowan Williams, *Lost Icons: Reflections on Cultural Bereavement* (Harrisburg, Pa.: Morehouse/Continuum, 2003), 148.

26. Job 1:22.

27. Job 2:10.

28. H. W. Brands, *Theodore Roosevelt: The Last Romantic* (New York: Basic Books, 1997), 165.

29. Doug Wead, *All the Presidents' Children: Triumph and Tragedy in the Lives of America's First Families* (New York: Altra, 2003), 353.

30. Brands, *Theodore Roosevelt,* 802.

31. Ibid., 803.

32. Ibid.

33. Ibid., 802.

34. Ibid., 803.

35. Richard Shenkman, *Presidential Ambition: How the Presidents Gained Power, Kept Power, and Got Things Done* (New York: HarperCollins, 1999), 81.

36. Ibid., 92.

37. Smedes, "What's God Up To?" 38.

38. Shenkman, *Presidential Ambition,* 92.

39. Doug Manning, *Don't Take My Grief Away* (San Francisco: Harper & Row, 1979), 47.

40. Job 5:17–18.

41. Job 5:25.

42. Job 42:10.

43. Chuck Johnson, "Sorrow and Memories: A Year Ago Darryl Kile Died of a Heart Attack. His Family, Friends and Teammates Are Still Learning to Cope," *USA Today,* June 17, 2003, C2.

44. Jane Stanford, at www.stanford.edu/home/stanford/history/begin.html #Jane.

45. Brands, *Theodore Roosevelt,* 163.

46. Albert Truesdale, "If God Is God, Then Why?" lecture, Kansas City, May 1, 1997.

47. Schaper, *Mature Faith,* 57

48. Ibid., 56.

49. Cathy Smedes, "Coda," in Lewis B. Smedes, *My God and I: A Spiritual Memoir* (Grand Rapids, Mich.: Eerdmans, 2003), 179.

You Have Permission to Hope (pages 127–146)

1. Susan Ford Wiltshire, *Seasons of Grief and Grace: A Sister's Story of AIDS* (Nashville: Vanderbilt University Press, 1994), 181.

2. William Gaunt, *Turner* (London: Phaidon, 1971), 17.

3. Genesis 19:24.

4. Garrison Keillor, *Prairie Home Companion* broadcast, May 11, 2003.

5. Eleanor Wilson McAdoo, ed., *The Priceless Gift: The Love Letters of Woodrow Wilson and Ellen Axson Wilson* (New York: McGraw-Hill, 1962), 315–16.

6. Ibid., 317.

7. Ibid., 316.

8. Arthur Walworth, *Woodrow Wilson,* 2nd ed., revised (Boston: Houghton Mifflin, 1965), 418, 436.

9. Christopher Hibbert, *Queen Victoria: A Personal History* (New York: Basic Books, 2000), 286–87.

10. Richard Hough, *Victoria and Albert* (New York: St. Martin's Press, 1996), 208.

11. Elizabeth Longford, ed., *The Oxford Book of Royal Anecdotes* (New York: Oxford University Press, 1989), 392.

12. Thomas Attig, *The Heart of Grief: Death and the Search for Lasting Love* (New York: Oxford University Press, 2000), 63.

13. Wilma Mankiller, *Mankiller: A Chief and Her People* (New York: St. Martin's Press, 1993), 226.

14. Ruth 1:9.

15. Ruth 1:20–21.

16. Beatrice Gormley, *C. S. Lewis: Christian and Storyteller* (Grand Rapids, Mich.: Eerdmans, 1998), 17.

17. Ibid., 20.

18. Thomas Attig, "Relearning the World: Making and Finding New Meanings," in *Meaning Reconstruction and the Experience of Loss,* ed. Robert A. Neimeyer (Washington, D.C,: American Psychological Association, 2001), 43.

19. Mrs. J. E. Theophilus to Dwight David Eisenhower, in *The Papers of Dwight David Eisenhower: The Presidency: The Middle Years,* vol. 15, ed. Louis Galambos (Washington, D.C.: U.S. Government Printing Office, 1996), document 1014, p. 1238.

20. Attig, "Relearning the World," 43.

21. Mary Higgins Clark, *Kitchen Privileges: A Memoir* (New York: Simon & Schuster, 2002), 116–17.

22. Ibid., 157.

23. Ibid., 204–5

24. Ibid., 111.

25. Frederica Mathewes-Green, *At the Corner of East and Now* (New York: Jeremy T. Tarcher, 1999), 57.

26. Ruth 3:1.

27. Gregory Orr, *The Blessing: A Memoir* (San Francisco: Council Oak Books, 2002), 14.

28. Ibid., 15.

29. "A Christmas Conversation," *Time* (January 5, 1987): 3.

30. Orr, *The Blessing*, 3.

31. S. David, "Once You Forgive, There Will Be Healing." *Christianity Today* (February 2003): 46–48.

32. Ibid., 48.

33. Norman Rose, *Churchill: The Unruly Giant* (New York: Free Press, 1994).

34. Cited in Eric Schlosser, "A Grief Like No Other," *Atlantic Monthly* (September 1997): 50.

35. Leonard Pitts Jr., "Grotesque Image of Segregation," *Kansas City Star,* January 14, 2003, B5.

36. Ibid.

You Have Permission to Name Your Loss
(pages 147–160)

1. Susan Sonnenday Vogel, *And Then Mark Died: Letters of Grief, Love, and Faith* (Nashville: Abingdon, 2003), 109–10.

2. Thomas C. Reeves, *Gentleman Boss: The Life of Chester Alan Arthur* (New York: Alfred A. Knopf, 1975), 190.

3. Ibid., 247.

4. Ibid., 159.

5. Genesis 2:19.

6. Gary Egeberg, *From Self-Care to Prayer: 31 Refreshing Spiritual Tips* (Mystic, Conn.: Twenty-Third Publications, 1999), 110.

7. Earl Cavanaugh, "Homily, St. Andrew's Episcopal Church," Kansas City, Mo., June 1, 2003.

8. Carl Sferrazza Anthony, *Florence Harding: The First Lady, the Jazz Age, and the Death of America's Most Scandalous President* (New York: Quill, 1998), 493.

9. Ibid., 491–92.

10. Ibid., 495.

11. Ibid., 497.

12. Jennifer Elison and Chris McGonigle, *Liberating Losses: When Death Brings Relief* (New York: Perseus Publishing, 2003), 152.

13. Ibid., 153.

14. Marc Gafni, *Soul Prints: Your Path to Fulfillment* (New York: Pocket Books, 2001), 110.

15. Egeberg, *From Self-Care to Prayer,* 111.

16. Carolyn A. Koons, *Beyond Betrayal: Healing My Broken Past* (San Francisco: Harper & Row, 1986), 3.

17. Ibid., 273.

18. Ibid., 274.

19. Ann Weems, *Psalms of Lament* (Louisville, Ky.: Westminster John Knox Press, 1995), 34

20. Genesis 2:19.

21. The Editors of Canari Press, *Random Acts of Kindness* (Berkeley, Calif.: Conari Press, 1993).

22. Tim Ghanni and Peter Cooper, "A Legendary Farewell to June Cash," *Nashville Tennessean,* May 19, 2003, 5A.

You Have Permission to Reinvent Yourself (pages 161–177)

1. Eleanor Roosevelt, *This I Remember* (New York: Harper & Brothers, 1949), 346.

2. Ben Bradlee, *A Good Life: Newspapering and Other Adventures* (New York: Simon & Schuster, 1995), 262.

3. Christopher Andersen, *Jackie after Jack* (New York: William Morrow, 1998), 89.

4. Jay Mulvaney, *Diane and Jackie: Maidens, Mothers, Myths* (New York: St. Martin's Press, 2002), 170.

5. Paul O'Neill, "For the Beautiful Queen Jacqueline, Goodbye Camelot, Hello Scorpios," *Life* (November 1, 1968).

6. See Martha Duffy, "Profile in Courage," *Time* (May 30, 1994): 28–38.

7. Robert A. Neimeyer, *Lessons of Loss: A Guide to Coping* (New York: McGraw-Hill/Primis Custom Publishing 1998), 96.

8. Ibid., 60.

9. David Roosevelt, *Grandmere: A Personal History of Eleanor Roosevelt* (New York: Warner Books, 2002), 59.

10. Ibid., 60.

11. Ibid.

12. Ibid., 97.

13. Ibid., 197.

14. Eleanor Roosevelt, *This I Remember,* 345.

15. In William Bridges, *The Way of Transition: Embracing Life's Most Difficult Moments* (Cambridge, Mass.: Perseus Publishing, 2001), 155.

16. Candice Carpenter, *Chapters: Create a Life of Exhilaration and Accomplishment in the Face of Change* (New York: McGraw-Hill, 2002), 39.

17. John Goff, *Robert T. Lincoln: A Man of His Own Right* (Norman: University of Oklahoma Press, 1969), 70.

18. Ibid., 71.

19. Ibid., 196.

20. Ibid., 262.

21. Eleanor Roosevelt, *This I Remember,* 345.

22. Elliott Roosevelt, *Eleanor Roosevelt with Love: A Centenary Remembrance* (New York: Lodestar/Dutton, 1984), 100.

23. Ibid., 345.

24. Geoffrey C. Ward, ed., *Closest Companion: The Unknown Story of the Intimate Friendship between Franklin Roosevelt and Margaret Suckley* (Boston: Houghton Mifflin, 1995), x.

25. David Roosevelt, *Grandmere,* 196.

26. Ibid., 197.

27. Elliott Roosevelt, *Eleanor Roosevelt with Love,* 104.

28. David Emblidge, ed., *My Day: The Best of Eleanor Roosevelt's Acclaimed Newspaper Columns, 1936–1962* (New York: De Capo Press, 2001), 100.

29. David Roosevelt, *Grandmere,* 197.

30. Elliott Roosevelt, *Eleanor Roosevelt with Love,* 105.

31. Ibid., 57.

32. American Hospice Foundation Telecast, April 30, 2003.

33. Walter Brueggemann, *First and Second Samuel,* in *Interpretation: A Bible Commentary for Teaching and Preaching* (Louisville, Ky.: John Knox Press, 1990), 218.

34. Mark 1:35.

35. Henri J. M. Nouwen, *Our Greatest Gift: A Mediation on Dying and Caring* (San Francisco: HarperSanFrancisco, 1994), 72–73.

36. Ibid.,73.

37. Phyllis Root, *The Name Quilt* (New York: Farrar, Straus, & Giroux, 2003), 22.

38. Robert Draper, "Papa Bush Lost His Presidency to a Southern Charmer: Is John Edwards the New Bubba?" *GQ* (December 2002): 285.

39. Ibid.

40. Ibid.

41. Nouwen, Our Greatest Gift, 72.

42. Roy Hattersley, *A Brand from the Burning: The Life of John Wesley* (Boston: Little, Brown, 2002), 389.

You Have a Right to Support from Your Family (pages 178–197)

1. Dawn Siegrist Waltman, *In a Heartbeat: A Journey of Hope and Healing for Those Who Have Lost a Baby* (Colorado Springs, Colo.: Faithful Woman/Cook Communications, 2002), 43.

2. Barbara Bush, *Barbara Bush: A Memoir* (New York: Charles Scribner's Sons, 1994), 46–47.

3. George W. Bush, *A Charge to Keep I Have* (New York: William Morrow, 1999), 14.

4. Susan Ford Wiltshire, *Seasons of Grief and Grace: A Sister's Story of AIDS* (Nashville: Vanderbilt University Press, 1994), 92.

5. Ibid., 189.

6. Arthur Ashe and Arnold Rampersad, *Days of Grace: A Memoir* (New York: Knopf, 1993), 50.

7. Edward Klein, *The Kennedy Curse: Why Tragedy Has Haunted America's First Family for 150 Years* (New York: St. Martin's Press, 2003), 149–50.

8. Ibid., 159.

9. James Robert Parish, *Rosie: Rosie O'Donnell's Biography* (New York: Carroll & Graft, 1997), 4.

10. Henry Fonda with Howard Teichman, *Fonda: My Life* (New York: New American Library, 1981), 204.

11. Ibid.

12. Ibid., 206.

13. Peter Fonda, *Don't Tell Dad* (New York: Hyperion, 1998), 45.

14. Peter A. Selwyn, *Surviving the Fall: The Personal Journey of an AIDS Doctor* (New Haven, Conn.: Yale University Press, 1998), 107.

15. Ibid., 106–7.

16. Ibid., 113.

17. Ibid.

18. Ibid., 115.

19. Doug Wead, *All the Presidents' Children: Triumph and Tragedy in the Lives of America's First Families* (New York: Altra, 2003), 345.

20. Jean H. Baker, *Mary Todd Lincoln: A Biography* (New York: Norton, 1987), 223.

21. Ibid., 220.

22. Ibid., 223.

23. Ibid.

24. Ibid., 224.

25. Jennifer Fleischner, *Mrs. Lincoln and Mrs. Keckly: The Remarkable Story of the Friendship between a First Lady and a Former Slave* (New York: Broadway Books, 2003), 267.

26. Baker, *Mary Todd Lincoln,* 225–26.

27. Lisa Beamer and Ken Abraham, *Let's Roll: Ordinary People, Extraordinary Courage* (Wheaton, Ill.: Tyndale House, 2002), 68.

28. Ibid.

29. Ibid., 72.

30. Dexter King with Ralph Wiley, *Growing Up King: An Intimate Memoir* (New York: Warner, 2003), 48.

31. Ibid., 49.

32. Ibid., 54.

33. Ibid., 61.

34. Ibid., 62.

35. Ibid., 74–75.

36. Ibid., 75.

37. Ibid., 84.

38. Ibid., 85.

39. Norma Zimmer, *Norma* (Wheaton, Ill.: Tyndale, 1976), 269.

40. Waltman, *In a Heartbeat,* 27.

41. Mark Hardt and Danette Carroll, "Divorce and the Death of a Child," *Bereavement* (May–June 1998): 6.

42. Ibid.

43. Susan Eisenhower, *Mrs. Ike: Memories and Reflections on the Life of Mamie Eisenhower* (New York: Farrar, Straus & Giroux, 1996), 73.

44. Carlo D'Este, *Eisenhower: A Soldier's Life* (New York: Henry Holt, 2002), 157.

45. Waltman, *In a Heartbeat,* 90.

46. Barbara Bush, *Barbara Bush: A Memoir,* 46.

47. Aaron Latham, "How George W. Found God," *George* magazine (September 2000): 80.

48. Ibid., 81.

49. Ibid.

50. Vogel, *And Then Mark Died,* 44.

51. Robert Dallek, *An Unfinished Life: John F. Kennedy, 1917–1963* (Boston: Little, Brown, 2003), 108.

52. Margaret Leech, *In the Days of McKinley* (New York: Harper & Brothers, 1959), 17.

You Have Permission to Remember Your Dead (pages 198–221)

1. Thomas Attig, *The Heart of Grief: Death and the Search for Lasting Love* (New York: Oxford University Press, 2000), 27.

2. Samuel R. Gardner, *History of the Great Civil War, 1642–1649,* vol. 4: 1647–1649 (New York: AMS Press, 1965), 322.

3. 1 Corinthians 11:23–24.

4. Anne Brener, *Mourning and Mitzvah: A Guided Journal for Walking the Mourner's Path through Grief to Healing* (Woodstock, Vt.: Jewish Lights, 1993), 78.

5. Ibid., 78–79.

6. Karen Uhlenhuth, "'More Dearly, Departed': Funerals Are Seeing an Evolution of the Eulogy," *Kansas City Star,* August 10, 2003, F8.

7. Jennifer Elison and Chris McGonigle, *Liberating Losses: When Death Brings Relief* (New York: Perseus Publishing, 2003), 76.

8. Matthew 18:20.

9. Therese A. Rando, *Grief, Dying, and Death: Clinical Interventions for Caregivers* (Champaign, Ill.: Research Press, 1984), 109.

10. Elison and McGonigle, *Liberating Losses,* 76.

11. Mark Twain, *Mark Twain's Letters, 1872–1873,* ed. Lin Salamo and Harriet Elinor Smith (Berkeley: University of California Press, 1997), 5:99.

12. Ibid.

13. John van Druten, *I Remember Mama,* in *Three Comedies of American Family Life,* ed. Joseph Mersand (New York: Washington Square Press, 1961), 8.

14. Alba Ambert, "Persephone's Quest at Waterloo: A Daughter's Tale," in *Las Mamis: Favorite Latino Authors Remember Their Mothers,* ed. Esmerald Santiago and Joie Davidow (New York: Knopf, 2000), 61.

15. Tony Walter, *On Bereavement: The Culture of Grief* (Philadelphia: Open University Press, 1999), 47.

16. Mary Higgins Clark, *Kitchen Privileges: A Memoir* (New York: Simon & Schuster, 2002), 130.

17. A. Niebergall and Gordon Lathrop, "Burial: Lutheran," in *The New Westminster Dictionary of Liturgy and Worship,* ed. J. G. Davies (Philadelphia: Westminster, 1986), 125.

18. Cited in Leon Wieseltier, *Kaddish* (New York: Knopf, 1998), 192.

19. Niebergall and Lathrop, "Burial: Lutheran," 126.

20. Brener, *Mourning and Mitzvah,* 137.

21. Wieseltier, *Kaddish,* 546.

22. Alfred J. Kolatch, *The Jewish Mourner's Book of Why* (Middle Village, N.Y.: Jonathan David, 1993), 332.

23. Rabbinical Assembly, *Siddur Sim Shalom for Shabbat and Festivals* (New York: United Synagogue of Conservative Judaism, 1998), 184.

24. S. J. Maslin, ed., *Gates of Mitzvah: A Guide to the Jewish Life Cycle* (New York: Central Conference of American Rabbis, 1979), 63.

25. Kolatch, *The Jewish Mourner's Book of Why,* 348.

26. Brener, *Mourning and Mitzvah,* 218

27. David Cressy, *Birth, Marriage, and Death: Ritual, Religion, and the Life-Cycle in Tudor and Stuart England* (New York: Oxford University Press, 1997), 400.

28. John Greenleigh and Rosalind Rosoff Beimler, *The Days of the Dead* (San Francisco: Pomegranate, 1991, 1998), 16.

29. Gina Hyams, *Day of the Dead* (San Francisco: Chronicle Books, 2001), 45.

30. Ibid., 53.

31. Ibid., 69.

32. Ibid., 72.

33. Ibid., 78.

34. Tony Walter, "A New Model of Grief: Bereavement and Biography," *Mortality* 1, no. 1 (1996): 9.

35. B. DeOre, "Saving the Memories," *Dallas Morning News,* August 2, 1998, 10J.

36. Amy Dickinson, "Family Legends," *Time* (May 31, 1999): 103.

37. Ibid.

38. William Gladstone, cited in *Respectfully Quoted: A Dictionary of Quotations Requested from the Congressional Research Service,* ed. S. Platt (Washington, D.C.: Library of Congress, 1989), 73.

39. Robert Dallek, *An Unfinished Life: John F. Kennedy, 1917–1963* (Boston: Little, Brown, 2003), 696.

You Have Permission to Keep Your Grief (pages 222–231)

1. Sally Higgins, cited in Harold Ivan Smith, *Grieving the Death of a Mother* (Minneapolis: Augsburg, 2003), 110.

2. Dr. Kenneth Playfair Duncan, *Times of London,* June 30, 1999, 24.

3. Kathrin Boerner and Jutta Heckhausen, "To Have and Have Not: Adaptive Bereavement Transforming Mental Ties to the Deceased," *Death Studies* 27 (2003): 200.

4. "Cosby to Return to Work Next Week," *Kansas City Star,* January 23, 1997, E7.

5. Victoria Alexander, *Words I Never Thought to Speak: Stories of Life in the Wake of Suicide* (New York: Lexington Books, 1991), 159.

6. Dan Mercer, "Why a Memorial?" letter to the editor, *Kansas City Star,* July 16, 2001, B4.

7. Judy Wieden, "The Shepard Family Heals," *The Advocate* (October 12, 1999): 41.

8. Ingrid Seward, *William and Harry: The Biography of Two Princes* (New York: Arcade, 2003), 225.

9. Susan Ford Wiltshire, *Seasons of Grief and Grace: A Sister's Story of AIDS* (Nashville: Vanderbilt University Press, 1994).

10. Chris Hedges, "An Unending Journey through Faith and Heartbreak," *New York Times,* December 15, 2002, sec. 1, p. 38.

11. Dawn Siegrist Waltman, *In a Heartbeat: A Journey of Hope and Healing for Those Who Have Lost a Baby* (Colorado Springs, Colo.: Faithful Woman/Cook Communications, 2002), 50–51.

12. The History of Widener Library at http://hcl.harvard.edu. widener/about/history/html.

13. David Hosick, "After a Child Dies," letter to the editor, *Christian Century* (June 14, 2003): 45.

14. Revelation 21:4.

15. *The Book of Common Prayer,* 364.

16. Genesis 23:2–3.

Acknowledgments

It is important to "give credit where credit is due." I am deeply indebted

To the fine scholars and clinicians who make up ADEC, the Association for Death Education and Counseling, who have befriended me during this writing project. Moreover, they provided significant opportunities for me to share initial findings with Association members.

To the American Academy of Bereavement, which offers me a setting in which to teach my historical narratives.

To the amazing librarians in the presidential libraries across the country who have helped me find and interpret documents. And to the fine reference librarians in the Kansas City Public Library System who have borrowed numerous resources for me for this project.

To Dennis and Beulah Apple and Andy Apple, who have modeled grief keeping following the death of their incredible son, Denny, in 1991. In a "get-over-it" "move-on" world they have taught me to keep the grief. Denny's death invited me to become a grief educator.

To my editor at the Crossroad Publishing Company, Roy M. Carlisle, who understood the need to grant permission for grief keeping and who said, "I want to publish this book."

About the Author

Harold Ivan Smith is a speaker, teacher, author, story-teller, counselor, and grief educator. A well-known thanatologist, he has special training including a Certificate from the Mid-America College of Funeral Service and certification by the Association for Death Education and Counseling, where he also serves on the National Certification Panel.

As a much sought after speaker, Dr. Smith has presented keynote addresses all over the United States and abroad, including for the National Hospice Organization's Conference on Pastoral Care, the Perinatal Bereavement Conference, the King's Conference on Bereavement in Canada, the Third World Gathering on Bereavement, the International Conference on Care and Kindness, and the National Funeral Directors Association. He frequently leads workshops for hospice training events and pastoral leadership conferences. Dr. Smith has pioneered the use of children's books with adult grievers, and regularly leads Grief Gatherings — innovative storytelling groups at St. Luke's Hospital in Kansas City. His many media appearances include guest spots on *The Hour of Power* with Robert Schuller.

Harold Ivan Smith holds a B.A. from Trevecca Nazarene University, an M.A. from Scarritt College, an Ed.S. from the George Peabody College of Vanderbilt University, and a D.Min. in Spirituality from Asbury Theological Seminary. Harold Ivan is an adjunct professor in the doctoral program at Northern Baptist Seminary and has taught courses in bereavement at Nazarene Theological Seminary, MidAmerica Nazarene University, and Bethel Seminary (St. Paul). He is a faculty member of the American Academy of Bereavement, offering continuing education workshops for clinicians across the country.

Harold Ivan has authored twenty books, and various editions have been published in Spanish, Korean, Afrikaans, Mandarin Chinese, and Indonesian. Dr. Smith lives in Kansas City, Missouri.

A Word from the Editor

Recently I was browsing through a pile of old photographs, as I am more wont to do as I grow older. It is an odd pastime I must admit, and the desire will surface at strange moments when I am wondering about this person or that person whom I have known over the years in some professional capacity. In this instance it was photos from almost twenty years ago. Usually I find interesting photos of someone whom I have not been thinking about, and that is what happened that day. Here in my hand was a photo of Harold Ivan Smith and me with our friend Carolyn Koons, a well-known speaker and professor at a southern California university, and various other people sitting at a dinner table at some conference. Harold Ivan and Carolyn were the conference leaders, and I was clearly enjoying our dinner conversation. It brought back the memories I had of Harold Ivan introducing me to Carolyn and the subsequent very mutually satisfying publishing experience that Carolyn and I enjoyed as editor and author. And it also reminded me of what I have noted throughout the years in my long relationship with Harold.

Here is a man who has an insatiable desire to know what is going on in the world. And the intelligence and wisdom to sort through all that comes his way. Here is also a man who has that amazing gift of being able to sort through incredible amounts of information and data and then present that abundance of ideas and experiences in compelling ways for any kind of audience, be it lay or professional. Here is also a man who will not sit still for injustice in any form and who will also not be led astray by the myriad con artists that populate religious and political groups ad infinitum. The sum of my deliberations was simple: here is one of the most interesting intellectuals that I have had the privilege of calling friend.

And, of course, here was a man who loved to write! But for reasons that now seem just idiosyncratic we were never in a position to work together as editor and author. Now with his twentieth book I was finally in a position to publish a book that I knew was incredibly important and that would make both of us very proud.

For the last several years Harold Ivan has taken on subjects that most of us try to avoid, death and grief, and brought to these subjects his own wise and deeply spiritual perspective. And in an even more specialized way he has researched the impact and power of grief processes throughout the history of the lives of U.S. presidents and their families. Most of us cannot even fathom how grief has affected, even changed the course of political life at the highest levels in this country. But you will learn some of that reality by reading this amazing book.

Finally, in his usual sagacious and comprehensive approach Dr. Smith now educates all of us — by means of this book and his peripatetic lecturing — about how we can all be healthier human beings by understanding the deeper dynamics of funeral rites and grief processes. It is my great privilege not only to publish this book, *GriefKeeping,* but also to introduce all of you to one of the more interesting and compassionate men I have had the privilege of knowing.

Roy M. Carlisle, *Senior Editor*

Index of Names

Of Related Interest

Mary Ellen Berry & Carmen Renee Berry
REAWAKENING TO LIFE
Renewal After a Husband's Death

In the tradition of the *New York Times* best-seller *girlfriends, Reawakening to Life* weaves together the stories of widows of strong faith who have found rebirth, celebration, and new identity after the death of a husband. The stories are a living example of how widows can grow deeper in their faith when they remember the strong ties of family, friends, and fellow believers.

0-8245-1978-7 $16.95. paperback

Please support your local bookstore,
or call 1-800-707-0670 for Customer Service.

For a free catalog, write us at

THE CROSSROAD PUBLISHING COMPANY
16 Penn Plaza, 481 Eighth Avenue
New York, NY 10001

Visit our website at
www.crossroadpublishing.com
All prices subject to change.

crossroad